THE
BOOK *of*
FREEDOM

A Channeled Text

PAUL SELIG

THE MASTERY TRILOGY:
BOOK III

A TARCHERPERIGEE BOOK

tarcherperigee

An imprint of Penguin Random House LLC
375 Hudson Street
New York, New York 10014

Tarcher and Perigee are registered trademarks, and the colophon is
a trademark of Penguin Random House LLC.

Most TarcherPerigee books are available at special quantity discounts for bulk
purchase for sales promotions, premiums, fund-raising, and educational needs.
Special books or book excerpts also can be created to fit specific needs. For details,
write: SpecialMarkets@penguinrandomhouse.com.

Library of Congress Cataloging-in-Publication Data

Names: Selig, Paul, medium.
Title: The book of freedom : a channeled text / Paul Selig.
Description: New York : TarcherPerigee, 2018. |
Series: The mastery trilogy ; part 3 | "A TarcherPerigee book." |
Identifiers: LCCN 2018004684 (print) | LCCN 2018029384 (ebook) |
ISBN 9781524705206 (ebook) | ISBN 9780399175725
Subjects: LCSH: Spirit writings. | Liberty—Miscellanea.
Classification: LCC BF1290 (ebook) | LCC BF1290 .B65 2018 (print) |
DDC 133.9/3—dc23
LC record available at https://lccn.loc.gov/2018004684
p.   cm.

Printed in the United States of America
3   5   7   9   10   8   6   4   2

CONTENTS

PREFACE

There is no real creative joy in delivering a channeled book. There is no real artistic satisfaction, because the words on the page are the words I am given in sequence, as fast as I can speak them with no thought of what follows next. There is no crafting of the manuscript, and no editing whatsoever except for the occasional mispronounced, garbled, or dropped word in a sentence that was spoken too quickly, and even those are exceedingly rare.

There is no personal thrill here and, oddly, when people come to me telling me how deeply these books have moved them, transformed their experiences of themselves and their world, I am happy for them but feel next to no satisfaction for a job well done. These are not my books. My name appears on the covers and, to that end, I feel a personal responsibility to be authentic in my questions to the Source of the teaching because I do not want to be participatory to something that could be confusing, or harmful, or too challenging to be known as true.

But my experience of what comes through me, again and again, is that the teaching is true, even when I don't comprehend it. I am not a spiritual teacher or guru and I do not want to be. I want no one's authority and the Guides that come through me say, also, that the true teacher is the God within, and they are here to show us the way to that so that we may know our own sovereignty and experience the divinity that is our birthright.

I understand, on a certain level, that this is true and so I have continued, lecture after lecture, group after group, to show up for this work even though I can't always say that my own life is necessarily a testament to this teaching. Perhaps one day it will be. I hope so.

I had asked about my role once in channel, when I had made one of my many inquiries about my own progress, my own perceived failings in the face of some of the teaching, my own challenges with weight, or loneliness, or the sense of separation I can feel at times from the somewhat more "normal" life I had lived as an academic prior to devoting myself full time to this work. The answer I had been given, right or wrong, was that my job, by my agreement, was to hold the door open for others and when they passed through, I could follow.

At the close of this book, the Guides welcome the readers of this text to a very new life. A very new awareness of their own divinity in form, a new understanding of responsibility for oneself and one's world. They call their students across the threshold, joyously, emphatically, to come and partake in what they call the Kingdom, described by them as the awareness of God in all manifestation. I have been invited now to follow, and I hope that I do and that I can.

The promise of this book, the sixth in a sequence of teachings on the evolution of consciousness and the realization of the divine in form, was made in the very first dictated text, *I Am the Word,* that was delivered through me over the course of two and a half weeks in 2009, "the Christ in man is an event that happens."

They say it has happened, is happening, and we are welcome to it.

The door is open. I hope to see you all on the other side of what we have known, to what we all may know and experience and discover on the other side of the threshold. Thank you all for being my companions on this strange journey that has been the delivery of these texts. The Guides say that there will be more.

> Blessings.
> Paul Selig
> On an airplane to somewhere, September 22, 2017

The following are the transcripts of channeling sessions recorded between July 30, 2017, and September 20, 2017, in workshops and seminars conducted in New York City, Boston, The Art of Living Retreat Center in Boone, North Carolina, Seattle, and the Esalen Institute in Big Sur, California. Selected student questions have been included.

THE CHRIST IN MANIFESTATION

Day One

Now when we teach you about what you are, you need to understand we are not making you do anything. We don't decide for you. We claim you as you truly are and you can go into agreement with that vibrationally in accord with us—vibrational accord, yes.

Now as you say yes to this teaching, you confirm it for yourselves in the lives you live. We don't give you permission to decide for us—why should you give us permission to decide for you? But we may confirm a choice that you will make, that the Divine as you is here as you, and we will say we can do this because it is always so. Do you understand this? It is always so. Agree to it or not, it is still so.

Now when we confirm you and we say your name—"you

are free, you are free, you are free"—we announce a truth, an ever-true truth, and you confirm it. The choice is yours to confirm. But by your confirmation you adapt and align to the vibrational intention that has been claimed for you. "You are free." Like it or not, agree to it or not, what else could you possibly be?

Now when you choose this, choose to move into accord, the life you live begins in increments to transform itself to the realization of truth that is ever here. To realize something is to know it, and while we know you are free, and the True Self that you are knows you are free as well, the confirmation of it has not claimed itself in manifestation as the life you live. And our confirmation of you, "you are free"—in encoding in the field you hold, confirmed by you as you say, "I am free" in confirmation to our claim—claims the field, the auric field, if you wish, in vibrational accord with what you have chosen. First the field must be assumed and claimed in this way, and then the life you live must move into accord to it.

Now each of you comes here with ideas of who you are, and in fact you wish them to be confirmed by us. "I'm the one who is always wrong, who never gets his way, who must be seen as special or in authority. I can never be wrong because my world would end if I am." These fear-based selves seek confirmation as well. And while we do not confirm them, we recognize them as exactly what they are—the mask of fear that you wear at the cost of the Divine Self, who is here and can announce himself at any moment. And in this announcement, what has been confirmed in fear—"I am not worthy, I will never be wrong"—must be encountered in a reckoning.

A reckoning, as we have taught, is a facing of the self and all of its creations. Everything you have claimed and chosen in fear surrounds you in the field you hold, and as you announce yourself as free—"I am free, I am free, I am free"—you actually transform the choice you have made in fear to the new agreement of freedom.

How can you be free if your idea of yourself is to be confirmed in a fearful way? How can you be free if others can decide for you who and what you truly are? How can you be free if your fear-based self is telling you every day that you are not going to get what you want?

Now, in fact, you may not get what you want because what the small self wants, in almost all cases, is confirmation of what she thinks she is. "I am the one that doesn't get her way. Confirm it for me and then I will be right." If you want that, if you want what you have had, you can have it if you want it. That is up to you. But we will not confirm it for you because, if we were to do that, we would have to lower our vibration to the level of claim that you are making, and we will not do that because our work is in a different way.

You may have your mother confirm who you think you are. She is probably the one who told you what it was to begin with.

"You will never get your way."

"Yes, Mom, I know."

And your world confirms it.

We agree to who you are, who you can only be in truth, and in truth a lie will not be held. And a lie, we would suggest, is the small self's claim about who she thinks she is, who he must be to get his way. We will not confirm this because it is not true.

Now the truth of who you are, the Divine as you, is nothing more, nothing less than the essence of the Divine that is instilled in you and in all things, that seeks its expression as what you are—underline the word *what*—the manifestation of the Divine as what you are in form, in field, and in expression. And that is new for Paul that we say it this way, the Divine as you in form and field *and expression*.

As you express as the Divine, you claim the divinity that is inherent in all things. By nature of your being, you claim what is always true, and your regard for the material realm that you have inherited transforms the realm in vibration to lift it to its true nature.

As we have said many times, a note that is played on a piano may exist in different octaves. You may play a note in a low octave or a high octave. You play the note in a high octave, you are in resonance with that note, and then this becomes your expression. If you see the gesture he* makes, we will call this the mudra of expression because the announcement of the Divine as you in expression must claim a world through participation in it.

This does not mean you decide where you should go to get what you want as you think you should have it. That is the small self commandeering this teaching to get what it thinks it should have. The Divine as what you are—underline *what*—in expression claims the world, not the small self with its dictates of what should be. You are told what to want and you agree to it at the cost of what might be claimed in a higher octave.

Now the frequency we operate from is the Christ, and that is a level of manifestation that may be undergone in form by each of you by your agreement. And by *agreement* we mean resonance, not just choice, but by the alignment that follows choice. "The Christ in Manifestation" is the title of this teaching, and we will confirm its use when we wish to. Whether it is in the text or not, it is our purview to decide what is in our books. And the Christ as you, while it has

---

*Paul.

xviii INTRODUCTION: THE CHRIST IN MANIFESTATION

been a teaching here, is widely misunderstood because you assume it to be a religious teaching, and it has never been.

The divine principle, the active principle of God, if you wish, in action, is called the Word. In the beginning was the active principle, and the manifestation of it in form is the truth of who you are. The alignment to this truth is another matter entirely. You have been gifted with free will. You assume yourself to be as you want, and you confirm your reality in consort with your fellows, who would in most cases have you agree with them.

"Oh, look at that terrible thing." "Look at that lovely man or woman."

"We will tell you what to desire, who you should be, and what you should agree to."

The True Self exists beyond conformity, and conformity is always to one thing—history. You are conforming to history by your acquiescence to it. By *acquiescence* we mean agreement again. "I will agree that this is a Sunday. Everybody says it's Sunday. I will not be the only one wrong."

Your decisions are based in history. "I should have this kind of a job, this kind of a practice, this kind of a mate. I should be seen in these ways because, if I am not, I am not in agreement to the history that I know myself through."

When you understand that the claim "I am free, I am free, I am free" transforms history by a new agreement, you can operate through the claim and begin to express as the True Self or the Christed principle in manifestation. This does not make you Jesus. We are not saying you are going to walk on water. But you are going to know your relationship to the Divine that is inherent in all manifestation.

The small self cannot know this, and that is why we bring this teaching to you now. The small self cannot know it. She cannot abide in the higher field because what she has known was claimed for her in an agreement to separation.

"Now what the hell does that mean," he asks, "agreement to separation?"

You are born in fear, in some ways, because you operate in a field that is in agreement to fear. This is not your fault. It is not original sin, and we say that for Paul who had a question in the back of the room. But you are born in fear—not the field you hold, but the confirmation of your field within the larger intention. The manifest world has been so in agreement to fear, it is an expectation of being.

Now if you imagine an infant, who knows its truth, suddenly thrust into a dense field that is fraught with fear and inherits the information that was created in fear, you have separation. The Divine that is the child is still as present as it ever was, but the confirmation of its reality has been confirmed by the collective, and the collective has decided what will be so.

Now the small self in most ways is an agreement in a collective, only because its agreements were made in a time where she was seeking to learn who she was. And what she learned confirmed the need for fear and for anger and for thoughts that she would not get what she wants because she is not worthy.

"Worthy of what?" he asks. Worthy of the Divine Self in full expression. *Full expression* is what we said, yes.

Now the idea that you will be fully expressed as the Divine Self is a point of great confusion for all of you. You think it means you will be taking bows. You will be so luminous nobody can gaze upon you. Your bills are paid for you. The beautiful men and women you desire are all present all day long because you are so wondrous. Or you assume that it means you become pious and separate from the world and deny yourself pleasure because you perceive the Divine to be outside of form and the idea of pleasure must be of a lower nature.

Neither is so. To be fully realized as the True Self, the Divine as what you are, requires one thing—to surrender to what you have always been at the cost of the known. "Behold, I make all things new" has been the teaching, and the surrender and acquiescence to the true nature of your being and its expression is what claims you.

"But what does this look like?" he asks. "What is the price we pay? Why would we want this?"

Here is the terrible news, Paul. It looks just like you are now, and the woman before you, and the gentleman in the back row. It looks just like them. Your agreement to what perfection means is also a product of the collective that would decide for you what divinity looks like—do you all understand this?—the Divine as you, as who and what you are and can only be. Underline the word *only.* Can *only* be. Everything else is an idea and nothing more—an idea that you are not worthy, an idea that humanity cannot get along, an idea that you are not one with the Source of your being.

The truth of who and what you are has come to be known. You are free. You are free. You are free. And as we announce these words—"you are free, you are free, you are free"—we welcome you to *The Book of Freedom,* and this is its introduction.

Chapter One

AGREEMENT TO THE NEW

Day One (Continued)

Each one of you comes with a question about who you are, an identity that needs to be released in order to be assumed by the True Self or that aspect of you that you may call the Divine informing all things.

Now what you think you are, in some ways, has been an issue. You are in a mortal body having an experience in a dense plane. And while we don't deny this, we will also suggest that your vibratory field can lift you beyond the density of form and field, as you have known it, to begin to exist in a higher octave. The teachings that you receive through us have been instrumental for some of you in a new regard of being, what it means to be. But the field that you hold has been imprinted, not only by us, but your history, your race, your culture in ways that must be released to support the new in re-forming you.

You understand the idea of freedom as being without history or not aligned to the old ideas that would ask you to conform to them. To be truly free is to be realized, and to be realized means to know. But if what you think you are is operating in limitation—"It cannot be so, I cannot be this, I cannot be realized"—you will confirm this.

Now the idea of realization must be understood for some of you. It does not mean you become enlightened, that you become the light of the world, as much as it means you become what you have always been in a realized state. Ascension for some of you has been described as bypassing physical reality, living on a cloud with the unicorns or the angels. And that is not this teaching. This has always been a teaching of value, and what you are is as valued as anything else. To preclude the what, which means the physical manifestation of form that you know yourself as, would be to lie. You are in a body, you are not the body, the body is of God, but it is not God itself. To preclude God from the body is to deny God in all manifestation.

The realization of the divinity of form comes at a cost. That which you would think you are and anoint yourself as will be released by you at the level you can handle or hold, the higher octave. The two notes may play concurrently, but eventually one note may take precedence. The small self existing in the low octave and the Divine Self existing at the high octave are operating concurrently, but with a predominant echo—and by *echo* we mean resonance, the resonance of your field, the obligations that you make in karma through form in the dense vibration, these things that you believe will always be there that will align to the small self at the cost of what would be brought.

The True Self, you see, is as here as well as it can ever be, but its expression has not been predominant as your expression. So the alignment to the self as what you are, the Divine in form and field, has been required because the exclusion of the form has excluded your embodiment. If the Divine does not exist in form, then you do not exist in form as the Divine. Do you understand this? It's very simple. The teaching of God in the heaven and you in the mud has rendered the mud without God when God can only be the mud and your skin and your breath and in the eyes of a child and the dying man, the God that is is implicit by its nature in all manifestation.

Now what creation is, in some ways, is manifestation. And every thought you think contributes to form. It doesn't necessarily make form so. You do not invent a million dollars in a bank account by thinking it today and expecting it to be there tomorrow. But you do agree to the manifest world through your thinking, and what you think of the world actually confirms the world that you see.

As the small self continues to claim the world in agreement to history, it continues to render in creation what has been as what will be. And there is an assumption here, an implicit assumption, that things will not change, that the Divine as you in its circuitous way must exist within a landscape that the small self has inherited. To do this is to deny the Divine in form as what you are and its expression as what it sees.

Now you understand the idea that the God Self, if you wish, can see the God in all things, that the True Self, if you wish, can see the truth in all things, but you don't understand that how it sees confirms what it sees in the manifest world. The divine principle that you are is expressing itself as a creative act and calling into being what it knows to be so, which is often contrary to the teachings of the small self. When the Divine knows the Divine in manifestation, it claims it into being as a creative act, and ideas of limitation that have been confirmed by the small self must be rendered obsolete.

How this is done is done in agreement to the new, and if this is in the book—and we are saying this for Paul, who is worried about this—we will call the chapter "Agreement to the New." The agreement to what can be known in the higher octave is what gives it permission to be made known in form. What is obsolete will be released from you because you cannot align to it anymore.

"Now what does this mean?" he asks. "I have things in my life that feel low that I would like to see changed. I have unhappiness and confusion and fear. What happens to these things? Are they eradicated?"

In some ways you rely on these things to tell you who you have been, and they seek to confirm themselves as what you are. In fact, you are not fearful and worried, but you assume yourself to be and then claim this in creation because you expect it to be there. As you begin to align to the what that you are, the Divine as what you are, and the claim is made through you—"I am free, I am free, I am free"—the field that you hold will move to embark upon the release of what no longer confirms this.

What we would like to say is that what you know as fear has been an agreement to be fearful. When you stop agreeing to be fearful, you stop aligning to fear—agreement to the new once again. "But I have always been sad," he says. Or she says, "I have always been alone. Will this change these things?"

In fact, they will. They will change if what you have learned through them has been learned to the degree that you no longer need to replicate them. The one who knows himself as fearful may learn the lessons of fear, but he need not learn them all his life. In some cases, a lesson in fear may be useful to the progression of the soul, but once you understand that fear is a liar and has no reason to be, the lesson has been learned and you need not claim it again.

The Divine as what you are actually exists in a realm where fear cannot manifest. If you really understand what this means, it means that you align to an octave or a level of vibration where the manifestation of the Divine precludes the expression of fear because fear cannot align to it. As you begin to align at this level, you become the expression of it, and by *expression of it* we mean you align to the manifestation of it in all you see before you. You are agreeing to be what you are at the cost of the old and herald the new by nature of your expression in it and how you perceive and what you claim.

If the fear self is not expressing, you cannot claim in fear, and as you do not claim in fear, you do not manifest. As you stop agreeing to it, you stop claiming it and making it so. In other words, friends, the idealization of the old, what you have known, what you have been taught at the exclusion of truth, has called a world to you that operates in fear.

Now as we sing your song for you—"We know who you are in truth, we know what you are in truth, we know how you serve in truth, you are free, you are free, you are free"—we announce the truth of your being, and consequently the field you hold in confirmation to this begins not only to eradicate fear, but to see it for what it is—a great liar. And, again, we say, in truth a lie will not be held.

As you stop confirming lies or agreeing to them, what you begin to perceive is a new field, a new world beginning to express that is operating outside of fear. This is a reality already. This is not something that is fixed. You are moving into another level of agreement with the common field wherein you lift it to its true nature, which does not align to fear.

This is world service, yes, but the idea of it is too vast for the individual, so we will do our best to claim you each in this teaching in a way that you can concur with and agree to.

Now how this is done is in attunement, and we will do this, not only for the people in the room, but for those who are experiencing these words wherever they may be, and we will announce them for you each as one. As we say these words for the collective, we move into agreement for the collective to resonate as what we say—underline *as*—the being as you in the common field, the collective field in a new agreement.

Here are the words we will speak for you all:

"On this day we claim that the ones we see before us, the ones in encounter with these words, will be known by us in the higher octave that they abide in. And as we agree to this, as we say these words, we confirm each one of them to align to their higher nature in embodiment. We know who you are in truth. We know what you are in truth. We know how you serve in truth. You are free. You are free. You are free."

Now as we intend to teach you all, we will also teach the ones who are not present and may never hear these words, and we will invite you all, you who read the texts, you who hear these words, to say these words with us to humanity, incarnation, civilization, in expression through individual intent, and you may say this after us very softly:

"I know who you are in truth. I know what you are in truth. I know how you serve in truth. You are free. You are free. You are free."

Now, if you wish, know that this is so, that humanity itself, every incarnated individual at its essence, is free in truth, that the divine nature of each, regardless of what he or she thinks, is as present now as it can ever be, and your claim of it in freedom is announcing its purview in humanity in expression.

"I know who you are in truth. I know what you are in truth. I know how you serve in truth. You are free. You are free. You are free."

Dominion, you see, is creation in action. And your dominion is to claim your world. But if you claim it as a small self, you incur what the small self needs to learn, and perhaps will learn through in a high way. But when you claim as the True Self, you claim love, you claim freedom, you claim truth, and its manifestation will teach you in wonder.

Day Two

We ask you questions about yourselves and the lives you've lived thus far. What have you chosen and why? "Why did I go to that school, take that job, marry that man or woman? Why did I believe myself to be capable of these things?" You chose them, you see. You encountered something and you chose it. And by doing that you created the potential of a potential reality being made manifest for you. In that manifestation, you learned and you encountered the questions that you require to take you to your next learning.

Some of you decide in advance what you will learn through

an encounter. "I will meet this man. He will tell me what I need to know." But most encounters offer an opportunity to know what you don't because you are not expecting it. The possibility that is inherent in any engagement far surpasses what your small self would decide you may learn from.

Each of you comes to this teaching with a level of awareness of who and what you are based on the lives you've lived thus far. And your encounter with your lives in many ways has claimed you with an identity that you use to navigate a reality. The small self, you see, has a great investment in replicating the known so that what he encounters is in alignment with who he thinks he is, and what he has chosen prior is what has given him that evidence.

As we work with you each, as we lift you past the old to what may be claimed, what may be known in a higher octave, we realize you outside of the claims made for you or by you by your parents, by your history, by the culture you were born into. In some ways, if you can imagine, what we are doing is lifting you up, gazing upon you outside of the known so you may have a window or a reflection into your eternal self at your eternal self's will. You engage in an encounter with the True Self that you return to the old with. The lifting itself acclimates you to the potential of the True Self as being realized, and then as you return to who you think you are, you have a new experience with yourself and your world.

The Divine as what you are has been this teaching so far, and the what in manifestation, the Divine as you in form and field—and, now, in expression—is the teaching of the text we write. The Divine as you in expression is how you serve and how you claim a world into being that exists in the higher octave that the True Self aligns as and with.

Now some of you deny the who and the what that you are. "I am a small man." "I am a needy woman." "I am an unhappy man." "I am an angry woman." And you confirm the identity because it's what you know, or because you believe you cannot release the old that has been so over-identified as you that it has claimed your world in manifestation.

Because you align to the old and you decide that it must be there, you witness it everywhere you see, and your confirmation of your small self—"I am angry or afraid"—will announce itself at every opportunity. As you realize the what that you are, the simple fact that the Divine as you is in form—not as an idea, but as a reality—you are confirmed in your reality because the vibratory field that you align as, as the True Self in manifestation, claims the world before him or her in like accord, the Divine as the Divine existing in a field that is also true, and by *true* we mean of God, or whatever you mean God to be as Infinite Source.

Now the what that you are has also been decided by the small self and conditioned itself in several ways to be realized in lower vibration. You decide what you are in almost all cases based upon the lists that you have had to choose from. "I am in a man's body." You can check that off your list. "I have a job and a title and I know myself as that." "The body that I am in is working or not, depending upon the list I've known and agreed to know myself as, and the body that I know will not be here one day and most likely end itself from this ailment that my mother had, or that ailment that did my father in." You prescribe your reality, and in many cases the body confirms the ideas you've inherited as well.

Now once you understand that the what that you are, which is the form you have taken, is as of God as anything else you could encounter, your realization of the body will begin to be confirmed by your expression. Now, this is very important to understand. Your expression, the field you hold in activation, is already manifesting the world you see before you. Everything you see you are in agreement to, you have given a name to. "That is my friend." "That is my house." "That is my government." And you are confirming what you see, individually and also collectively—"our country," "our way," "our inheritance." The idealization of everything you see, as pronounced by you, is historical data making itself manifest by your agreement.

So if you understand now that the small self, individually and collectively, is accountable to everything before it, which simply means in alignment to because you perceive it, and because you perceive it are informing it by consciousness to claim it in one way or another, you will begin to realize that your expression as a what, the small self as what, is dictating the reality you see. As you align to the Divine as what you are, the manifest *what,* what you begin to understand is that what is claimed by you will actually confirm the divinity that is inherent in you. The truth of who and what you are manifests here and realizes the truth in all you see before you. What realization is, is knowing, and to know the truth in anything is to realize it.

Now the manifestation of God as you must be understood in several ways so you don't run screaming from the room as you toss the book aside. The Divine as what you are is your true nature. Underline the word *true.* Your true nature has been expressed by you in some ways, but in most cases your true nature has been operating in a dense field, operating in fear. And your attempts to realize yourselves in action have in many ways been circumvented by the collective that says it cannot be so.

Now the Divine as you seeks its purview, and its purview

is simply the responsibility of realization as who and what you are, for your own highest good, yes, but most importantly for the good of the species, the good of the echo of your emanation as the True Self in the collective field to establish the new that seeks to be born at the cost of the old. The Divine as you is here. She has always been here, he has always been here, but her realization has been hindered by your agreements to the collective of what may be known in possibility.

Now alignment, as we have taught you, is accord— a-c-c-o-r-d or a-c-h-o-r-d as on a piano. You are in vibratory accord with everything you see. It could not be there without you, individually and collectively. The chord that is played aligns you to what you see, and the collective chord that has been playing is in fact something you all attend to—with variance, yes, and we will attend to this later—but in vibratory accord you all know your world.

As you align to the True Self, the Divine as what you are, the God Self, if you prefer, its achievement is its realization as and through you, at the cost of the old, that would claim a new world into manifestation. "What kind of new world?" he asks. "Are you speaking metaphorically? Are you speaking in symbols? Are you speaking about the world we live in?"

We are speaking of the world you live in, because how you

perceive anything claims it in manifestation. You call that man ugly, and you have made him so. You call those people evil, you have made them so. You decide that this is worthy, you have made that thing worthy. And the small self's directives become a shared construct. "We all think they are evil, we all think he is ugly, and we all will decide what will be, based upon the data that we have inherited."

As you realize the True Self, the True Self perceives the man that was ugly is beautiful, those that you thought were evil hold inherent good that seeks to be realized, and the world before you must—underline *must*—begin to reflect this consciousness, because consciousness manifests in form. The what that you are is the manifestation of the Divine as you, and its expression claims the world in high accord. What the Divine Self then claims is the Kingdom, and the Kingdom as we have described it—the realization of the Divine in all things, the knowing of the divine template that is always present in manifestation—confirms a new reality, and by your very presence, you are lifting your world in high accord.

Now as we teach you each, we comprehend your difficulties. We don't make you wrong. You can learn through anything you like, high and low and in between, and you will still be loved, individually and collectively. But the species that you are is seeking realization at the cost of the old, and your permission is required here—you who hear these words, you who may read them on a page, your permission is required. If you are not willing to release the ideas you've held that have operated in fear—have been your teachers, perhaps, but still seek to control you—you will not lift beyond the matrix of collective fear that has established itself very seriously in this plane.

The alignment to truth which we have brought forth prior, the agreement to be in truth with the comprehension that in truth a lie will not be held, was the prerequisite for the text of freedom, because you cannot be free if you are in fear, and the control of fear would do its very best to deceive you and mandate a new world that is in agreement to its choices. You are aligning above what has been claimed for you, through this work. You are lifting above limitation that has been prescribed for you, through this work. And if you agree, if you give permission, if you say yes, we assure you that what you will receive is the wonder and the beauty and the alignment to the Divine that you have required to release all that has been controlling you or telling you, you are not allowed.

The gift of this teaching for some of you will be small. "I realized I was free to choose in certain ways when I assumed I was not." And if that toe is in the water, that is a fine thing. You will get ready to swim when you are ready. But the truth of who and what you are seeks realization, and, with your permission, it will take you into the middle of the ocean and say, "Yes, we are here, we are here. Not only do we swim, we fly. We are free, we are free, we are free."

Those of you who say yes—who say, "Yes, I may, yes, I may choose, yes, I may know, yes, I may agree to the truth of what I am" so that this truth may be expressed in fullness— may claim a new world. Those of you who say, "No, I will not, I cannot, I am too afraid to let go of the ideas I have held to encounter myself in a higher way" will learn in other ways, and that is also fine. Humanity itself makes its choices, and the agreements that will be made now, in the years to come may well change the course of humanity in a high way. If you all agree, it can be made so.

We are here to shepherd you. We are here to teach you. We are here to lift you, as we said, so that your true reflection may be known to you so you may return to your world with a new idea that may be born in fullness.

We will continue this teaching after a pause. We have one thing to say to Paul. Yes, in fact, this is the continuation of the chapter, and we thank you for your presence in delivering it. We will say this, as well. You are not to alter the text. We have never altered the text, so you must trust the transmission is the perfect transmission and will be comprehended in perfect ways by anyone who encounters it.

We will lastly say this. We are very grateful to those of you who attend to these words. You have come to be known. You have come to be sung. And as we sing with you, we say, "Yes, you are here, and you are free." Period. Period. Period. Stop now, please.

(Pause)

We're ready to continue and we have a few things to say about realization and what realization means. The identities you've held seek realization in small ways. These are not bad things, but you have ideas about what you should be and how these things should play out. "I want this relationship to work. I want this career to happen the way I think it should." And you may learn from these things. You will progress through any encounter. But true realization comes at the cost of the old, and the identities you have held, small ways and high ways, must be encountered in this transformation.

Each encounter you have with any human being gives you an opportunity to know who you are, and perhaps know who they are as well in a higher octave. In order for this to occur, you have to stop identifying them as you think they are. Your idealizations of who anybody else is decides for them who they are, and *decides for them* means in small ways. The truth of who and what you are seeks realization in a new way, and the old way stands before it as a doorway that must be passed through and left, finally, once and for all.

"What does this teaching mean?" he asks. We will give you an example. You meet a man. He looks a certain way. You decide who the man is based on what you were taught to believe. You emblemize him or name him through the history you have claimed and reduced him in this manner. The small self may also idealize another. "Look at that wonderful man and all the good he does." You decide who he is based on your idealization of him and claim him in a way he may not be in truth.

As you realize yourself in a higher way, you are called to see your world in a higher way as well. And the guarantee we offer you of what this will be will be a way to know in any instant who another is because you are knowing them outside of the frames they have used or you have called to you that you would seek to place upon another. When you are free of the emblemizations that you have used to decide who others are, you are free to know them in a new way. When you are free to know them in a new way, you may have a new experience. But ninety percent of your encounters, we would suggest, are about you deciding who someone is and then seeking to confirm your idea for them. You get to be right all the time, which is just the way the small self likes it.

As you realize the what that you are—and we must explain this more for Paul, who is confused—as you realize the what that you are, you cannot help realizing the what that another is as well. Now, as we have said, *what* means manifest. To be a what means to be a thing in form, in manifestation. Your decisions about what form is in some ways has emblemized form just in the way we explained you emblemized others. You emblemize something, decide what it is at the cost of what it might be otherwise. And realization of form, the manifestation of the Divine as what you are, comes at the cost of the old ideas that you have decided must be so because that's what it has always been.

If you can imagine that the species that you are in and living as is resigning to what it has been at the cost of what may be known, you would understand that you are in fact limiting the evolution of the species that is here as well. You understand that there are ways to be outside of what you've claimed thus far. People may know things that they could not know without reason. People may see things in the energetic field that must not be visible in a lower vibration. But you really don't understand that alignment is the key here, and in alignment in the higher accord these things may be understood and are not so special at all.

You have been playing keys on a piano in a very limited scale. The piano keys exist in lower chords, in higher chords, in chords that may never be heard by the human ears. But the chords that play are the only chords you can hear and you

assume that will always be the case. As the species transforms, you have access to those things that exist in higher
octaves because you have aligned to that level. As you align to
that level, you give permission to everybody else to do the
very same thing. In some ways, your song, which is your expression, which is how you serve, becomes the benediction
upon all you see.

Imagine that there was a man who was a hundred feet
tall, a beautiful man with blue skin and silver hair. Nobody
has seen such a man, but the moment they do, they realize—
which means know—that such a man may exist. And suddenly you will find that people may be growing to a hundred
feet tall with silver hair and blue skin. Nothing may be claimed
until it is first claimed in possibility, and the possibility that
you have been operating in a limited field by collective agreement must be attended to now.

As you decide to be with us, you are already in an encounter with us, and in some ways you may look at us as the blue
man with the silver hair. We should not exist. This encounter should not be happening. But it seems to be so, and because it does, this may be so, and because this may be so,
many other things may be so as well.

The alignment you hold today has called your entire life
to you. Do you understand this? Your energetic alignment,
in its expression, has claimed your world and your experiences

in accord with you. The agreement to be realized as the who and the what that you can only be in truth has reclaimed your identity, and the field that you hold is now navigating your process for you outside of the historical edicts. You have already made the decision to move beyond the known to claim a new potential, and because you have said yes—"Yes, I am willing, yes, I am choosing in a new way"—you must count on the potential that you have chosen to be realized as and through you.

When you decide as a species that you can know yourselves in love, you will no longer harm one another. When you can decide that you don't need fear to be your teacher, you can move beyond the agreements you have made to it, but you have made many agreements in fear that you don't even know.

Take a moment now and think of four things that you were taught to be fearful of—what your mother said, or the church said, or your teacher said, or the married partner said—what you agreed to in fear. And then ask yourself another question: "How has my life manifested by agreeing to these things?" You will be very surprised at what you see. Some of you still don't talk to strangers. Some of you still fear that if you step on a crack on a sidewalk, your mother will be broken. Some of you still think that if you tell the truth, you will be hurt, and that it is safer to tell a lie to protect yourself.

But you don't know that the repercussions of these choices are actually informing your lives and teaching you through the repercussions of them.

If you are not choosing in fear, then how are you choosing? Paul is saying, "I don't know. How am I?" If you are not choosing in fear, you are choosing in several ways. You are choosing out of habit—"I have always done it this way, so I expect I will continue to"—which is historical data. You are choosing out of expectation. "I am expected to be this or that, so I will act in accord to it." Or you are choosing in reason. "If I choose this, that will occur. If I choose that, I will have that experience."

Now as you begin to operate as the what that you are, the Divine in form and field, how you choose begins to transform as well. Because you are not aligning to habit out of recourse, because you are not choosing in fear, because you are not doing what's expected of you—and while you understand reason, you also understand that the small self thinks and the True Self knows—you begin to bypass the history that has claimed you and claimed your choices for you.

The alignment you hold does not take away choice. It simply aligns choice in the vibration of truth. Understand what this means, friends. To be in alignment to truth informing your choices means you don't choose in fear, you are not operating in history, you are not operating in a reliance on reason, but in alignment to the True Self, who always seeks expression and will say yes to that which it requires to realize itself through.

The Divine Self as what you are seeks realization and will call to her or him whatever is required for this to occur. If that means breaking the window that has kept you indoors, or shattering the mirror that holds a distorted reflection so that you may know truth, that may be the occurrence that you encounter. But understand, friends: The Divine seeks to teach in love, and you always have the encounters you require to learn through. Although they may not seem in love, they may be great gifts once they are comprehended for what they truly are.

Each encounter, as we said, is a possibility to know the Divine. When you decide who you are in encounter based upon others' expectations for you, you diminish yourself and you go out of truth. To be in alignment to truth claims you and your encounter in a higher octave.

The agreement you will make with us today, if you wish, is that each encounter you have may be in alignment or agreement to truth. Do you hear these words? If each encounter you have is in alignment or agreement to truth, you are not bound by history or expectation or reason—and, we would promise you, you are not choosing in fear.

We will take a moment now and pause this teaching. Period. Period. Period.

(Pause)

Now when we teach you about manifestation, you must understand that you are already doing it. Everything you see before you is in vibrational accord to you, individually and collectively, and the claims you make in fear are called to you just like anything else.

Now this is not to frighten you. Because you thought a spider would come does not mean the spider will come, but it does mean that you are in alignment to that spider in expectation. The requirements for transformation of these things that you have claimed in fear, or expect will always be there with you in the causal field, must be understood by you first in order for them to be transformed.

As you live your life, you have many encounters. They are all your teachers, as we said. When you prescribe an outcome to any situation, you are expecting what will come and creating definition upon the situation that you seek to realize. You often do this in limitation because your ideas of what can be made known are very limited. When you align in fear, and begin to expect in fear, and claim outcomes in fear, you are delineating an outcome of a situation that you have decided is fearful. This is the key. You have decided it's fearful if a relationship ends. You have decided it's fearful if your child doesn't do what you think he should. You have decided it's terrible if you lose your job, or if she loses hers, or if this government topples, or that one rises. You have embellished these things with identity and meaning, just as you do the people that you see and decide upon, as we said prior.

Now the instruction you will receive here is about releasing fear. But to look at fear first and foremost as an energetic field, while supporting this, will not be nearly as beneficial to you as understanding that what you claim in fear has been decided by you, and because you've decided that something is frightening and have an investment in its outcome, you have claimed an identity in consort to fear.

"What does that mean?" he says.

"I am the one who is fearful. I am in fear, which means in the vibration of fear." Because you are in these places in the identity or field, you are in alignment to fear, and as we have said many times, the action of fear is to claim more fear. To release the identity—"I am frightened, I am fearful"—does not mean you deny a situation. But perhaps it does mean that you don't emblemize the situation as a crisis or as frightening. Do you understand this?

"Oh, my God, I may lose my house" is the frightening name the one who claims for himself in the face of a fire. "I am afraid. I am losing my house." You are less afraid of losing your house than what could happen if you do. And your idealization of what your life would look like as a homeless human being decides for you how to create a scenario in expectation. If you understand, each of you, that everything that you think is so important in your life is simply temporary and always has been, your attachment to the house, or your idealization of what it means to have a home, may be transformed.

Now as we teach you about identity as the fearful one, you must understand that there are choices to be made. Paul is not agreeing with this teaching thus far. "There are things that we are frightened of. We have a nervous system. We go into reaction. To be scared out of one's wits is less a decision than a reaction."

Well, once again, we would suggest that is historical programming, data you have used to know your world, and its response in being is fearful when it is triggered. The True Self, the one that you truly are, is never afraid, and you must understand what this means. Your over-identification with the small self, and what she has taught to idealize and also to be fearful of, has claimed these problems, whereas the True Self is always the solution to them.

Now when we say these words to you, we hope you understand that we are not telling you you are wrong if you are afraid. You may be taught by fear in constructive ways. You may learn a lesson through a fearful encounter. But we would invite you to understand that if you think that lesson is to stay afraid, you are lying to yourself. Every encounter is your teacher, and the claims that you make about the encounter prepare you for your next one.

As you create a life in accord with the Divine Self, you stop choosing in fear, and you also stop agreeing to it when it is offered to you. Your idealization of outcome—"I could lose my job, I could lose my house, I could lose my marriage"—in all ways is presupposing that there is an outcome that will be harmful to you. But if every encounter is your teacher, then every situation is, as well, and the liberation that may come to you, the new opportunities that may come to you through these changes, may be worth all the gold in the world.

If you understand that each idealization that you bring to any encounter has its data in history, and you have been taught to be afraid of this or that, or like this or that because you have been taught its value, you can begin to understand that, in almost all cases, what you witness is based on what you witness informed by history at the cost of what it truly is.

Imagine, for a moment, that there is a man standing in the front of a room. You can look at this man and assess his merit by his clothing, by his hair, by his manner, perhaps by his speech if he were to talk to you. Everything you have decided about this man was based in history, what you were taught to identify. He has new shoes on his feet and a fine coat—he must be a prosperous man. He has a shifty gaze—he must not be trustworthy. He is a very handsome man—he must be admired. He decides things for other people because of his demeanor, and your relationship to this man has been established for you by all of the codification or emblemization that you have given him.

If this man were to stand before you naked, you would decide other things. If you were to put poor shoes upon this man and a ragged coat, you would assume him to be something other. If you would decide that the one you see before you, regardless of what he's been seen as, is the Divine in form and can only be this, you will understand who he is beyond any of the significators that the small self would use to claim an identity for him.

As some of you come to us seeking instruction, you are seeking validation for who you are as a small self. "Tell me I am doing it right." "Tell me I am worthy of this journey." And while we may say these things to you, you have emblemized us and are acting in fear, in some ways, that your journey is not under your own purview as a True Self, and in fact it is.

The requirement of fear has always been to be what it is

in any form it can take. The masks that fear wears are already known to you in obvious ways, but the significant ways that it can sneak in are occasionally misunderstood. You don't understand that manipulation is fear, but manipulation takes many forms, including acts of kindness that are only present for one to get what he or she needs. You don't understand that fear may mask itself as glorious. The victor decides who wins and crushes the one who is defeated, but the idealization of the victor comes at a cost. The one who is a victor needs someone to defeat, and to be the one defeated is to be in agreement in a lower octave. Once the victor realizes that true victory is equality, and the games that one plays in competition are only games, and no one wins, and everyone wins, you can begin to live in a world that operates in peace.

Some of you decide that what it means to be a man or woman is to be in fear because you were taught by those who encouraged fear. If you are not afraid, you will be harmed. "Stay alert, stay on guard, be very careful who you speak to, who you let close." "Do not go into the light. You may be burned by the sun." These are teachings in fear, and if you have adhered to them thus far, you have paid the price for them.

To begin to comprehend that the what that you are, the Divine Self in manifestation, does not collude with or align to fear, you will understand that the True Self exists beyond it. And every encounter you've had with fear has been an encounter in lower vibration.

As we teach you about freedom, we want you to understand that freedom from fear and all of its masks will be paramount to this teaching, but the True Self, who is already here as you, doesn't need to fight fear because he can't exist at that alignment. The way to bypass fear is to lift above it to the self that cannot agree to it, nor ever will.

As we take a pause from this teaching for the day, we will thank you each for your invitation to learn, because as you learn and integrate the teachings we bring, we are enabling ourselves to continue. We write the book in preparation for the students who will receive it, and as they integrate the information and operate with the teaching, we continue to bring them what we may.

We are here for the students of this work in several ways. We usher you through the passages the text would bring you. We escort you around the corners when you cannot see what is before you. And we champion you in ways you may never know by singing your song for you when you forget the words to the truth of who you are.

We know who you are, and we always will. We know what you are, and we always will. And your service, we suggest, your contribution to this world, is an echo in the resonance of your expression, which is the text you read now, your expression, how you serve, and the alignment that is required to deliver you from fear at a collective level that would seek to distort the value you only have in truth.

We know you are here as you say yes, and as we say yes, this journey will continue. We will say that this is the end of the first chapter. Period. Period. Period. Stop now, please.

Chapter Two

THE ECHO

Day Three

Some of you decide prior to incarnation that you will realize yourselves, and you come with steps, encounters, opportunities to support you in this. Some of you decide that this may be the lifetime where you claim an identity that was waiting in the wings. The True Self has come, you see, and he has been waiting in the wings, she has been waiting for her cue, and the truth of who and what you are is present now and attending to you in preparation for her realization as who and what you are.

The changes you have undergone through participation in this teaching have claimed a life for you in ways you may not yet see. The preparation for this work happens in the energetic field, and your availability to transformation, in most ways, is what supports the changes that will be known through you and by you in the lives you live. Your attendance to the teachings, in several ways, support this happening. The first thing that happens is you begin to agree to a concept. "I may be more than I am, or more than I have known myself as." And as this is understood and integrated by the small self, opportunities arise for the small self to begin to claim her identity in consort with the possibility that there is much more to her than perhaps she has ever known.

The gateway is present then, through potential—through possibility, yes—to re-create the self in the octave that the Divine Self expresses through. Now, *express through*—we wish you to understand this. You are always expressing. The aspects of you that you have claimed in history are expressing themselves today. You all showed up wearing clothing. You all have clocks upon your bodies somewhere. There are ways that you've conformed to what you think you should do or be, because you think you should do to be.

Now when we teach you about the gateway to the True Self and how it presents itself, you must understand that the True Self is present. She is not to be sought. He is not to be looked out for as if he is just around the bend, or she is waiting for you somewhere else. When we said *waiting in the wings,* this means she is with you and as you. And her announcement "I am here, I am here, I am here," which we have previously explained in prior text* is the True Self announcing its purview, she only seeks to be known and aligned to and as, so that her purview is claimed with you. Underline the word *with*.

Imagine you are going on a date with your True Self. You have things you expect from any encounter. "I want to be treated well. I don't want to be told what to do. I want to feel as if I am valued." Can you understand, friends, that the True Self does these things? She is not out on a mission to exterminate you, and, in fact, at the end of a lifetime she will be holding the small self's hand and taking the bow with her for the life well lived.

The True Self, you see, incorporates the small self—perhaps, you could say, absorbs it—but not at the cost of identity. The True Self's identity has a name: I Am. And the I Am self may be known by you by the name you were born with, or any name you could choose for yourself. "I am ugly, I am happy" are ways of claiming identity as well. And the names you give yourself you claim coherence with and identify through, and they claim your world with you just as much as the True Self can.

When you realize yourself, which simply means know yourself and know who and what you are, the gateway is no

---

* *The Book of Mastery.*

longer present because you have stepped through. You have not abandoned the small self, but perhaps you are deciding that your realization at the cost of the known, those things you thought you were, will be claimed by you in a way that will support a life of recognition of the Divine in mastery in all you may know and see.

The claims we have made with you thus far in prior texts have been sequential. In our first text, we anointed you and aligned you to the Divine Self through the acclimation to the vibration of the Word. The Word, as we have announced it, is the energy of the Creator in action. This is the attunement to the Word:

"I am Word through my body. Word I am Word. I am Word through my vibration. Word I am Word. I am Word through my knowing of myself as Word. Word I am Word."

This is a claim of truth, and your alignment to these claims supports the energetic field, the body itself, and the identity you have known yourselves through in acclimating and realizing the vibration of the Word as who and what you are. As the radio that you are is attuned to play this station, you are in broadcast as and with it, and you may claim it for another—"I am Word through the one I see before me, I am

Word through all that I may know and see"—in a way that you may encounter in vibration. The palpable frequency of the Word may be known through you. "I am Word through my body. I am Word through my vibration. I am Word through my knowing of myself as Word."

When we claimed you later, we supported you in a new claim of identity:

"I know who I am. I know what I am. I know how I serve."

This supported the energetic field in reclamation of identity and field in an alignment to the moment you may know yourself in. When the True Self knows she is worthy, when the small self accepts the True Self as the aspect of her, she may claim these words: "I know who I am." The True Self announces the claim of truth. The small self is not able to, but she aligns to it in her field, and her form begins to agree, which means the systems that you know yourselves through are complicit in this alignment to the high vibration.

When we claimed you in knowing—"I know who I am"—we are speaking again of realization. The small self does not know who he is. He has done his best, but his purview is the purview of inheritance and logic, what he has been taught to believe and see. The True Self's purview—the

Divine Self or Christed Self, Eternal Self, if you prefer—the purview of the True Self is everything she encounters in the knowing that all is of the truth.

Now we will say this for Paul because he is questioning in the background. The small self's purview, while in fact it is everything she sees because the consciousness she holds is informing everything she sees, is limited in its expression because she has not aligned to the level of vibration or awareness of who and what she is. When the Divine Self witnesses something, she claims it in a higher way. When the small self witnesses something, she claims it as what she has been taught it is.

Now when we teach you in the claim "I am free, I am free, I am free," which is the claim of this text, you may begin to understand that everything that has preceded it has been in preparation for this level of adjustment to the True Self in its purview in all manifestation.

In the last text we wrote, we attended to form. *The Book of Truth* was a text on manifestation as the True Self and the alignment to truth that is now required to participate most fully in your embodiment in realization of the True Self. And the claim "I am free" has great power. This is not the same claim as the small self saying, "I am free of that ugly coat I threw out." "I am free of that friend who never said anything nice to me." The True Self, in its claim of liberation, supports the field, and then, consequently, the life. The one who claims it is living in the release of any and all attachments made in history that are operating in fear and limitation, and your expression, the expression of the True Self as what you are, must be realized through this claim.

The thunderbolt comes with the awareness that you have always been free, but your limited self, in its ascriptions to what she has been taught, has been denouncing her freedom at every opportunity. "I can't do this. Look at that person over there. She said she was free and she lost her husband. Look at that one over there. He said he was free. He is in the madhouse. I don't want freedom if it means losing what I have."

True freedom is the requirement of the Divine Self, who has released the need to conform to institutional policy, rhetoric, decisions made for him or her by others that would limit the soul's true expression. It is the release from all the alignment that you have confirmed by nature of being born in a field corrupt with fear that you have enjoyed and agreed to. The freedom that we speak of is the freedom of and from fear and all those things that it has wrought. And the realization of the True Self in manifestation, as who and what he is, is the equivalent to the rising of the Divine Self as a resurrected being. Understand the word *resurrection*. She is announced, he is announced, as the Divine Self in realignment to his true inheritance, her true nature. The Divine as you has come. She is here, he is here, and you say, "Yes, I am here, and I have come."

Now the small self would seek to acclimate this teaching to her personal needs. The small self would like to say, "Well, I always knew I was God. Why didn't anybody agree to me when I said I was? People should be doing what I say. Now, they have to." That is the claim of a fool and one who seeks to decide that her divinity is a pin she wears for others to admire.

The Divine Self, as we have said many times, could care less what anybody thinks of him or her. She is free. She is not operating from the dictates of fashion or culture or equivalence that she may have inherited, depending on where she was born and in what year. The Divine as what you are will not be appropriated by the small self.

In some ways, you may say, there is a mechanism that has been lifted to support this happening, and that mechanism will go back into place when you decide to appropriate a teaching such as this for the small self's aims. We will explain this. "I am a divine being" is a claim of truth. You may say this at any moment and it will always be so. And your resonance as this vibration, the one who knows who she is, will be met with a life in consort to the holding of the high field that the individual may manifest as.

The moment that same being decides that she is the only high being, the mechanism goes back. In some ways she shuts the door. It is still true she is a divine being. That will only always be true. But her decision to keep herself in separation supports the fear that is the mandate of separation, and she will be lying to herself if she claims to be the Divine Self in consort with others. The aspect that is this already is still present, but if you can imagine that the music was playing in the other room and she just shut the door to that room to seek some specialness and align her divinity to her personal mandates for what she wants.

You have understood surrender in some ways, but the truth of surrender is acceptance, acceptance of the self and all aspects of the self, because nothing can really be moved until it is aligned to and allowed to be moved to a higher way. If you accept another, like him or not, agree with him or not, you can go into an agreement with who and what she is outside of the small self's prescriptions. If you judge another, you have every right to believe that you judge yourself in the same fashion. And if you give permission to the True Self to support you in this way, you will find very quickly that you can know yourself without judgment with the support of the aspect of you that would find it impossible to judge.

You must understand this, friends. The True Self does not judge. She does not fear. She does not speak ill of her fellows. She does not speak ill of her small self, either. Why would she? How would she be a friend and an ally if she did such a thing? The Divine as what you are, in manifestation as you, will realize herself at the cost of the known—underline *will*—and that does include aspects of the self that are out of alignment, weeds in a garden, if you wish, that are prohibiting her from her full manifestation.

But as the weeds are pulled, the blooms appear, and all that is really being released are those very things that have kept the Divine Self from its full expression. And we do those things to support you in your realization of who and what you are so you may not be frightened of the pulling of the weed that you have lied about. "I am not an angry person," says the angry person. "I am not prideful," says the prideful woman or man. There is nothing wrong with those things, but they stand in the way of the divine expression.

When you accept that they are there, you can attend to them, but the True Self as you will attend to them far better and in perfect ways than the small self could ever manage. While the prideful man may become aware of his pride, he will not eradicate pride. He has no ability to do that. The Divine Self certainly does because the Divine Self is not prideful, and his manifestation comes forth in purview. The pride that he has known will be reckoned with, faced, and seen, in order to release so that the True Self may come forth in full bloom.

The travesty of mankind is that you think you are not divine. "Travesty or tragedy?"*

Travesty. We will speak to the tragedy in a moment, if you keep interrupting. The travesty of mankind is that you deny the divinity that is your inheritance, and you do this in collusion with your fellows. It's as if there's a terrible game being played upon every soul when she is incarnated.

"Welcome to the world! Do you know you are separate from everybody else?" "Welcome to the world! We are so happy to have you! Here are the things you should watch out for and fear."

And you say this to your children and to your neighbors, and then you legislate this behavior in your laws and governance, and then you war with each other and you wonder why.

"These are the things you should be afraid of."

"Watch your back with that one."

"They want what we have. We must make sure they do not get it."

Now, by *travesty*, we mean it's a charade. Finally, it's a

---

* Paul, interjecting.

charade. The entire idea of separation is an idea that you have manifested, believed to be true, but it has never been true. And the alignment as the Divine Self that you know yourself through in regard to this frequency may now be known in a way that will liberate you from the travesty and end the charade of separation once and for all.

The claim "I am free" is announced by the True Self. We do it three times for every aspect of being that you may know yourself as. Just as we said, "I am Word through my body, I am Word through my vibration, I am Word through my knowing myself," the thrice announcement "I am free" aligns every aspect of you to the high truth that is present as you in this agreement to be free. Did you hear that word? *Agreement* to be free. When the True Self claims "I am free," he goes into accord with all that may be known in freedom. He begins to align a life to the True Self, who is not in conformity operating as and in fear, does not seek to judge others because she knows the foolishness of it, and announces herself as free for the good of all humanity.

As each of you begins to express at this equivalent—the octave of freedom, if you wish to call it that—the vibration you hold in the field you know yourself through is emblazoned and visible in the higher identity of the I Am self, and may be seen and known in the fields and by the fields of everyone you encounter. In some ways, you become the gateway that you have already passed through. It has been said that "no one comes to the Father but through me." If you understand a metaphor, we may suggest that the Kingdom itself is on the other side of the gate of the realization of the True Self, and as you are realized, the vibration you hold can support your world in its own lifting. The vibration of the True Self in full realization is the manifest Christ, the Divine Self, the Eternal Self in form and field, and, finally, we say, in true expression.

If you can imagine that, simply by being in this octave, the field that you hold can support manifestation through your realization of what you see. We will give you an example. The one who knows who she is by nature of being, not through effort, knows who everybody else is as well. She cannot deny the divinity in anyone or anything because that is how she is known, and all she must know is in consort with that. Through the knowing of another, the other is lifted in vibration to a commensurate octave. The octave is present, the one in the high octave sees the truth in the one in the lower, and because she does, the field of the other meets the high, and in that communion you bear witness to truth at the cost of the known. "Behold, I make all things new."

Now you are not fixing people. You are not gazing upon them so that they do better things. You are simply knowing them—capital "K," know—and realizing them just as we realize you when we witness you and we say these words to you: "You are free. You are free. You are free."

If you wish to imagine us standing before you, however you may decide to look at us, whatever face you wish to bring as us, see us standing before you, and if you are willing, we will say this to you in form and field and expression: "You are free. You are free. You are free."

And say this in response, if you wish, and we will be in attunement to you, alignment with you, resonance as and with you to support you in this claim: "I am free. I am free. I am free."

Now be as you are, and know that this is so. The True Self is here. She is free. He is free. We know who you are. The small self will do its best to convince you you are not, but you know the truth—capital "K," know, which means realize.

We thank you for your presence. We will pause. Period. Period. Period. Stop now, please.

(Pause)

Some of you decide what your lives will be, what lessons will be learned prior to incarnation, and then assume, once you are born, that you made the wrong decision. "How did I get in this family? Why was I born in this culture? Who would choose this?"

Everything, as we have said, is an opportunity to learn

through. You are the one that decides, in some ways, what is good or bad, and any value you give anything claims the thing you've claimed value for in the ways you've prescribed. You all think this is a good thing because somebody said that it's a good thing. "Oh, how lovely; he got the job," and this is the job he will hate for the rest of his life. "Oh, lovely, she got married, finally; we never thought she would," as she enters her miserable marriage only to find out that she was much happier when she was alone.

You define outcomes based upon the expectations of the culture you live in. In the culture in America, the idea of status has ruled for so long that the hierarchies are implicit and unspoken. What is happening in this country now is the articulation of injustice in ways you have not seen yet, not for some time. The articulation of injustice is the speech that is made before the form. It is the announcement of the oppressed as no longer willing to stand in silence and allow the oppressor. But the issue that you will all be facing is how appropriated you have been collectively to structures of oppression, how you have agreed to it by ignoring injustice.

When you realize that the culture that you are living in here in this country has been appropriated by ideologies that you would never have confirmed intentionally, you will begin to decide to be free of even government, as you have known government. In our last text we said that everything will be changing, and everything will be, but not as the small self would have it be. The ruination of a system may be required for a new system to be born, just as a house must be leveled that has been eaten by termites and has a leaky foundation before the new foundation must be poured.

You are facing these times now, and we say congratulations for this. As we said, a reckoning is a facing of one's self and all of one's creations, and rule in fear, rule in distortion, rule in economic control, rule in religious control will all have to be attended to in the coming years for your species to evolve beyond what it's created thus far.

Now we don't say everything you've created is terrible. How could we say that? But what we are saying is you are complicit to your environment. You are complicit to the institutions that you complain about every day. You are complicit to religion. Now religion itself is not a bad thing, as long as it doesn't direct people and tell them what they are allowed. The foundation of each religion is in truth, but in most cases the diamonds of truth were poured in a mortar of distortion, and the institution itself and the bricks of the building it stands in are informed by the distortion, although the diamonds are still present if you look for them.

The acclimation you have to the lives you live now, and will continue to live in complicit nature, will be changing very shortly. You cannot ignore what is in front of you, and like it as you wish, what is before you will not be in your choice in a conscious way, but may well be what the collective has called forth to know itself through. Now when we teach you freedom, we teach you collective structures and your acclimation to them so you may move beyond them. If you don't understand that you are complicit to what you see—which simply means that because you are here with them, because you witness them, you are partaking in them and informing them energetically by your consciousness—you cannot understand that how you hold anything in vision supports what you see and in the ways you claim it.

The Book of Truth announced this, in some ways, as what was, as what you have inherited, and *The Book of Freedom* seeks renunciation and liberation from the collective fear that has been established here and is seeking, once again, to mandate who you should be and how you should live.

When a culture realizes itself as liberating, everything that exists within the culture may understand liberation. But each culture on this plane is still informed by the action of fear, as was prescribed for it. If you believe that your safety as a country is predicated upon the weakness of every other country, you are operating in fear and will seek to suppress the liberation of every other country. "But we don't like what they do, we don't believe as they believe, and we must be right, we have to be right, to support the identity that we collectively agree to."

If you understand that, even in that reasoning, you are giving permission to kill or to ignore or to suppress, and doing this in self-righteousness, you will begin to understand that the requirements of the identity of the country is to move into an agreement of love. "Now how does a country move to love?" Paul doesn't like this teaching in the least. He hopes it's not in the text. He doesn't want to hear these things. "A country in love. What a ridiculous idea. A country is an institution or a collective agreement, yes?"

In fact, what a country is, is an idea, and an idea that has taken form. And the agreements the country makes that take form you may understand as your mores, your economic systems, the laws you adhere to, and the government you build. But the idea of the country, in any case you can imagine, has been emblemized by an idea. "We are a country of warriors, we are a country that is superior to everybody else, we are always right" are ways a country may know itself. Or "We are always oppressed, never seen as valued, and consequently must make ourselves valuable through war or economic systems so that we may at least participate in the game that is being played elsewhere."

A country in love sounds implausible to Paul and a recipe for disaster. "The one with the open heart will be killed first.

There is no armor to shield the heart from the sword that would pierce it." When we teach a country in love, we are not teaching emotional love as you have been instructed in it. We are teaching love in the higher way, and the awareness of the Divine that may be known in love has no border, and the only laws it has are to support the well-being of all who live there. A country without laws may be known as lawless or violent, but if a law is made to oppress, to serve those with funds and defeat those with none, if a law is made for the rich at the cost of the poor, you have injustice, and finally, we suggest, you will have revolt.

The laws that you require in a country are collective agreements that you may follow to support the well-being of all. There is nothing wrong with paying a tax if the confirmation of the tax is for the good of the whole. There is nothing wrong with feeding your neighbor if your neighbor has no food. In fact, it is highly recommended that you do so. But because you were taught scarcity and continue to agree to it, you will not take from your plate and put on another plate what you think you need for yourself.

A country in love would not debase its neighbors. A country in love would welcome them. A country in love would not be in fear, because fear and love do not coexist. If you idealize love and make it something pretty or romantic, you will confuse yourself. "But we need borders," you may say.

"We need laws that keep people out." You need laws that include and instruct and support and teach. You need love to make these things possible, and when love is behind a law, the law will always be just.

"But mustn't there be penalties for an act against the whole, from one man against another?" Perhaps, yes, but penalization is seen as negative and not instructive, and until your laws support instruction and not incarceration, you will always have the problems you've had. Unless a man is seen in dignity, he will not be rehabilitated. And if you don't believe that any human being can be rehabilitated, you are missing the point of divinity. There is an aspect of the Divine even in the most miserable human being, or even the most violent, that can be recognized.

We are not asking you to be foolish. We are not asking you to walk into the cave with an offering for the man who would shoot you. But we are asking you to know the man in the cave as worthy of the light so that he may be led to it. What you damn, damns you back. And the truth of your being, the Divine as you, would seek to liberate all it sees because the Divine understands freedom.

The claim "you are free, you are free, you are free" may be said to anyone—underline the word *anyone*—and it will still be true at the expression level of the True Self because the True Self cannot be incarcerated, is not hidden in a cave, and the recognition of it that you may bring to anyone else will support their realization of their inherent freedom.

The truth of your being recognizes the truth in everybody else. Requirements are made by you to support fear, and as you decide to release fear, you release the requirements of it. The choice that you will make today, as you encounter these words, is to realize the self in a country of love. Wherever you experience these words, you are in a collective field. Understand this, friends. A community is a collective identity. A place of business is a collective identity. A state or a province also holds identity. And the country you live in, wherever it may be, also has an identity or an energetic field that is incorporating all that is within it and aligning to other energetic fields. Just as you imagine an individual with an auric field, you also may imagine a country.

Now while we are still speaking of individualized consciousness and collective consciousness in individualized ways—a community or a state or a country—you can also understand that those individual consciousnesses are expressed as part of a larger field, a communal field, a global field, if you prefer, even though that itself would be reductive because the globe itself that you know yourself on is actually part of a much greater system, and you can't even limit yourself by the species or planet you know yourself on. The agreement to be in a country of love may be claimed by you each for the benefit of the whole. Underline the word *benefit*. This does not mean that things look as you think they should. You are not making the world prettier. You are not saying no to this or that. You are claiming a truth when you claim these words, and these are the words we would offer you:

"On this day I choose to realize myself in a collective field of love. The collective field of love exists beyond any illusions of fear or separation that my small self might endow it with. And this collective field is connected to a larger field that I understand as my community, and then my country. As I align that the being that I am is in support of the whole, I can claim the liberation of the country I live in, and, in fact, the whole civilization of the world as in liberation. And here are the words I will use: You are free. You are free. You are free."

The claim "you are free," spoken to the unified field, the business place, the community, the state, or province, or country, or globe itself, will have its echo. Now the one who claims these words must be in the agreement to their own liberation, to their own freedom, for it to be so for others. But this does not mean that you must be in realization to do it. To be in agreement to something is to be in co-resonance with it, and the attunement you received earlier—"I am free, I am free, I am free"—has brought you into resonance with the claim we make for you. You may make this claim to another individual—"you are free, you are free, you are free"— or to your world.

Your realization that every human being upon this globe, like them or not, agree with them or not, is of God, or whatever you want to call God as, claims the truth, the very, very truth of their being. And that being, as you know, is free. Now we are not necessarily speaking of freedom from economic strife, although we would say that that can be seen as a creation of fear. We are speaking of liberation on a high level, and the knowing of the True Self in its full expression, which cannot align to the violence or fear-based choices that have been made throughout history to define a culture, or a country, or a community, or perhaps even a family.

The claim of liberation is always true at the level of the Divine Self. You do not have to say, "Well, why should I say they are free? They are not free. They are living in a regime that has no freedom." You are not claiming what they have. You are claiming what they are at their level of essence as an aspect of God with a Divine Self expressing itself in freedom.

Imagine you are lighting a match and holding it above your head. Imagine the fact that this light exists, ignites the flame that is held in everybody else, but you must hold it, and hold it high. You are free, and the lights light up around the world.

A community in love is a community without fear. A country in love is a country that does not debase its fellows, which is an act of fear. The prison doors must be opened to a new way. The wars you've claimed through an identity in violence must be re-known in a new way. If you are to continue to the starving of your brothers, the excluding them from care that they require must be ended for this community to survive. What you damn, damns you back. What you put in darkness calls you to it, and you enter the cave, that dark cave we described earlier where the violence awaits you because you have claimed all in violence. A community in love, a culture in love, does not harm, does not shame, does not starve, does not exclude any of its members. It heals and teaches and supports change in love, and, as we said, in love there is no fear.

We will stop this lecture for now. We may continue later. We may wait for another opportunity. We thank you for your presence. Stop now, please. Period. Period. Period.

(Pause)

Now when we teach you each about who and what you are, we don't exclude ourselves. You must understand this. The Divine as you is the eternal self. The aspect of you that knows who she is knows what she is as well. The truth of your being in manifestation, the Divine Self as what you are, is who claims the Kingdom, and we honor this. We reside in the Kingdom, in some ways, which means abiding in the presence of the Divine in the face of all things, all else that may be claimed.

While we don't deny the divinity in you, we also honor the humanity and that you have come to learn and create opportunity to realize yourself through. Who you are in some ways, at this station, is the ambassador of the Divine Self who inhabits a dense plane, and as the ambassador realizes his job to be in some ways a bridge between the octaves so that she may support the welcoming of others through the gateway, she also realizes that the being that she is operates in a high realm, and we are in this high realm to support you in your awakening and the claims that may now be made in a high way.

The understanding of the what that we are has been an issue here. Are we divine beings, ascended masters? Are we Melchizedek? Are we the Christ? The way you would delineate the who that we are in most ways would seek to conform to what you want us to be. Are we your angels? Are we your Guides? In truth, we are the True Self, the highest self that may be known in manifestation. As we were once in form, and most of us were, we learned the lessons of this plane and we assumed ourselves, as a result of these lessons, in a higher octave to support the evolution of humanity. The Melchizedek tribe or priesthood, if you wish, is sequential. We are always present on this plane in this work. We have agreed to it and we do this for our own benefit as well.

Our realization of this plane in manifestation of the Kingdom or Christ consciousness as available to all and present as what you are has been our calling, our instruction, our reason for being in this encounter for as long as there has been time. There have been civilizations existing on this planet prior to what you know. We were there and participatory to them. Many of the teachings of our times were sacrificed, or lost in the sands of time, in the ruins of things that will never be found again. But the consciousness that we hold is still present. The frequency that we hold has been emboldened in many ways by the transition of this plane that you live in. And the echo of our teaching throughout the decades, throughout the centuries or millennium, is as present now, but may be heard by those of you who are willing to say, "Yes, it will be so."

We have done this work through Paul before, whether or not he knows it. And the trials of his lifetime, in some ways, are the repercussions of having chosen this work again and again and again at the cost of the world that would say no to it or call it heretical. We have come in this lifetime with him to complete our work, as it may be completed with him, and for you as well.

The treatise you are receiving here will not be our last text, but the last of the series on incarnation as the Divine Self, which has been this teaching from the beginning. As we continue, we have much to discuss, not only about who and what you are, but who we are, as well, and what may now be known as the history of the plane that you exist in reveals its truth, unburies its secrets, and the resurrection of the Divine reclaims all things.

History, in some ways, is an idea—your idea of who you've been based on the photograph you see. "I remember that day. I wore the blue dress. He wore the beige shirt. We assumed we were happy." You remember the day and you give it meaning. History works in the same way. You are told what happened, and you are told what to agree to. Your idea of the history of this plane is so limited, we could not begin to teach you the truth of it in one sitting.

The manifestation of man on this plane, while you have been here for some time, has not been the only manifestation here or consciousness available to be known as, or what, or as a thing that has lived and existed. Your prominence on this plane, the who that you think you are as a conqueror, as an enlightened being, whatever label you would give yourselves, is in some ways the product of realization, but in most ways the product of fear. If you are not the conqueror, what does that make you? If you are actually in control of everything, what does that leave somebody else?

The confusion of identity that man has taken on throughout the millennium is actually being countered now through the claim of the True Self. If you understand the real meaning of "I know who I am in truth," you will understand this teaching completely. In the true claim of "I know who I am in truth," you are claiming your true history, not only as an individual, but as an aspect of a species and as a divine being. And everything that is not true, every illusion, false reflection, misguided way of perceiving, must be encountered, or reckoned with, or recognized, and be moved so that the true claim may be known. "I know who I am" claims what you are not, and the faulty history, the faulty ideas, the embellishments made throughout time in doctrine, in theoretical teachings that have become religions, must be understood as what they were and not what they are in truth. The True Self as what you are has very few questions about identity. He knows who he is. He does not need to be told or acknowledged as what he thinks he is because he knows.

Now when the True Self manifests in form, he does so at cost. The identity that's been held that was structured in history, agreed to in fear, must be re-known. And the passage you all undergo as a requirement of this teaching is the releasing of the old self. This does not mean there is not a small self. It means you are not seeking its confirmation. You are not dictating your life in its mandates, and its mandates have been all historical information that you have agreed was true.

"I know who I am in truth" renders this as what it is— ideas, thoughts, fears, appropriations in history that you have assumed to be yourselves. When you know the what—"I know what I am in truth"—even the physical self, the Divine Self in form which is the truth of your being, must undergo a passage. It is not a passage you would imagine, and it is not a passage in identification. It is a passage in physical reality. The assumption of the Divine Self as what you are in manifestation must reclaim the body in a very different way than you would assume. It can no longer align to fear, or the genetics you believe you have that cannot be transformed or realized in a higher way.

The principle of humanity as being static—the form that you have taken will always be the form you know yourselves in throughout history—is being rendered new. If the species itself is in transformation, the acquisition of what you are, the Divine in form, must be party to this. To understand this, you need to realize that God, or what you might call

God, is in all manifestation, but has been ignored as such. As you say, "Yes, this is what I am," and you move into this agreement, form itself is divinized, is known as what it truly is and can only be.

"I know how I serve in truth." This is the text you are reading now. How you are in truth, what you are in truth, how you express as truth in freedom is the text you are reading now. When you know what you are and you know who you are, your expression can only be what it is, and the expression of the Divine in form as you and all you see before you must be comprehended as "I know how I serve." The ability to be at this level of frequency bypasses the selfish needs you may hold, bypasses the reasons you may want it, or the issuance you think it should have or be. The ability to be as what you are, the truth of your being in form and field in expression, is the claim we make with you. And the alignment you have through this instruction is what will support you in this.

Some of you decide prior to incarnation that you will awaken, that you will know what you are. Some of you come to learn other things. One is not a higher choice than the next. Do you understand this? That would be the small self saying, "Look at me. I am the first in my class to awaken. Where is my gold star?" The one who came to stumble has given you the great opportunity to lift him to his feet. The one who has come to learn through illness has given you the great privilege of nursing him or her to health. The one who has come in illness of the mind or spirit is actually teaching you that humanity may express itself in vastly different ways and still be worthy of love and rejoicing and care.

Some of you believe that what is not pretty is not of God. Tell that to the snake in the grass. Tell that to the spider or the bat. Because you have vilified them, you have put them out of the light. But they are as joyful in their expression as anything can be. The same is true for your neighbor. Know him as who he is outside of what has been prescribed for him, and you may know God.

The divinity that we hold is the divinity you hold as well. We are less separate from you than you think, but we do have a mission—to realize you so you may realize yourselves and realize your world. If you will grant us your permission, we will attend to you in all ways, but not the ways you may want. You want your lessons to come through convenience. "Here is a nice afternoon. Bring me a nice lesson so that I may grow and learn. But when this afternoon is over, I don't want to look at it again."

Again, the small self seeks to realize itself through opportunity that is convenient to its identity. "I will learn rejection from someone I don't care about." That's a nice way to learn a lesson. You understand this. What a nice way to learn that you don't care what somebody thinks about you when the truth of the matter is you didn't care anyway. That's not very difficult.

When we say we support you in your lessons, we actually mean we support your ability to claim them in the highest way you can. Perhaps the easiest way is the highest way, so don't anticipate struggle or strife. Say instead, "I am here to learn. I am here to learn. I am here to learn."

The one that knows everything, or thinks she should or does, will not like this teaching. It will not confirm her small self. But if you are not here to learn, what are you here for? The teacher herself is a student of her life. She must be in order to be a fine teacher.

When you understand that a realization is knowing truth and identifying through it in alignment—"I am knowing myself in truth, and I am knowing this being, this situation, this opportunity"—you may progress rather quickly. Freedom, we suggest, is what you come to when you stop pretending that you are not free.

The last thing we will say before we pause is, "Yes, this is in the text." Thank you, Paul. And thank you who are here today to be in support of this transmission, and also to tell you that what we are imprinting this text with in the vibratory field that it will carry to the reader is freedom. And the ambition of freedom is to realize itself in every encounter.

So say yes to it, and let the book sing to you. "I am free. I am free. I am free."

Stop now, please. Period. Period. Period.

Day Four

Some of you have choices to make about what you will do after this class. "Will I go home? Will I go to a new life? What will I be and how should I choose when my entire life has been chosen for me?"

Some of you will decide to leave what you have known in ways you will not understand until the leaving has been done. You will not comprehend the choices you have made here in this class until you see the results of them play out in your life. If you have made a claim at any time in your life, it has played out in a script, of sorts, that you have agreed to. Every choice that has been made by you—high, low, and in between—has its own repercussions.

The claims we make with you here in several ways will manifest in your life. Until you know it, you will not know it has happened, and we will explain this. The claim "I am free," the claim of the True Self in expression—that is the claim "I am free"—announces itself first in your field, the vibratory field you hold. As it is announced there, in some ways it responds to the individual's requirements for what freedom is and how it can best be expressed. So you are being talked to in all ways through the claim "I am free." The announcement you make, "I am free in energetic accord," moves the field to an acquiescence to its new name: "I am free." And the amount of response that you can carry and hold and be expressed as and through will be claimed by you in the choices you will now make.

Some of you decide that what it means to be free is to go by a new name. "I will claim a new name." "I will look a little different." "I will get a different job." You are not free. You've made some changes, will learn through those changes. Perhaps you realize you are free to change your name or your wardrobe or your place of employment. But that is not freedom. You are still operating within the extremely limited scale you have inherited about what it means to be free.

The power of the claim "I am free" will not be known to you in fullness until it is made so, and announced in form, and the form itself has gone into an agreement with the manifestation of it. We will explain this. When something is claimed in the field—"I know who I am in truth," a claim in the field and a claim of truth, we have to say, because that claim is always true at the highest level—the energetic bodies begin to go into co-resonance with the claim, and in all ways they begin to distill the essence of the teaching of the claim as if soil is receiving a seed that must be grown. So the expression of the claim—if you wish to look at it as encoding in the energetic field that the energetic field now responds as, or planting a seed in the soil that will then express—you would have the same kinds of metaphor for a simple action. What is claimed in the energetic field must become manifest through form.

Now you hold form, you are in agreement to be in a body, you operate in form in most ways in your obvious interactions. "I will have lunch with this friend." "I will pay that man the money I owe." The manifestation of your choices from days past surround you now. The home you live in, the spouse you have taken, the names you gave your children were all choices in manifestation, and these choices set ramifications through the world. The child named Sarah behaves rather differently than the child named Cassandra. Sarah may do one thing. Had Cassandra been named, she would have done something rather different. You bought this house and not that house, and the infidelity with the neighbor's wife would not have happened if you had bought the other house.

Every trajectory of every choice ripples beyond the obvious. The spouse of your neighbor, who releases his wife and then goes off to have three more children with yet another spouse, claims other people into manifestation on this plane, and then the world is changed by their presence. You don't understand, yet, that even when you smile at a stranger, you may have changed the course of history. You do not see this, but you will when this life is ended and you witness your life as you have claimed it. You will realize that the response to that one smile saved someone's life, offered him an opportunity, perhaps, to make a different choice than he would have. He was going to leave his spouse. The smile reminded him of his spouse's smile, and they stayed together forever after.

Every choice has a response, and the claims you've made, through our instruction, in the field are now manifesting in form, which is why many of you are having experiences with the vibration or visual phenomena that you have not had as yet. Some of you believe that these are tricks of the eye. "I saw a light go off over that man." "I looked at that woman and she appeared to be a puff of smoke." What, in fact, is happening is that you are starting to realign to the higher octave, where form, as you have understood form, is beginning to manifest with your senses intact to respond to them in a new way.

Now the claims you make—"I am free, I am free, I am free"—call a response into action. The Word, as we said, the energy of the Creator in action as who and what you are, has been the foundation of this teaching. And the claim of freedom—true freedom, we suggest, beyond your idealizations of it—claims a life in a new coherence. And the fabric of your life, as has been chosen by you in the past, must be made new for the new to claim itself in form and field.

Everything before you that you have chosen in fear must now be responded to in a higher octave. You say you want this development, but you are too afraid to leave the choices of the past. You say you want transformation, but your idealization of what transformation is actually prohibits the actions that might give it to you. You say you want love, but you run from it because you can't understand that your agreement to be here in form also gives you the right to claim yourself as worthy of love. The Divine as what you are, the manifest self, knows what she is, and she is not afraid of love. The Divine as what you are, manifest in form, is not afraid of change. Why would he be? The Christ has come as each of you.

Now we will tell you what this really means. The aspect of the Creator instilled in you at the conception of your soul in realization and full expression is the Christed Self, or the Resurrection, if you wish to call it that. The Resurrection comes at the cost of what has been claimed and identified through in a fear-based way. You cannot collude with fear, you cannot embrace fear, you cannot direct others in fear and expect to know the Kingdom. We have taught this prior, but we must say it again. The Kingdom is the purview and the inheritance of the True Self. The small self cannot exist there, simply because she cannot align to it. She is not being punished by not stepping into the Kingdom. She still has too many bags that she refuses to release that would grant her entrance if she released them. The True Self as what you are—underline *what*—carries no baggage.

So much of our work with you has been in re-identification—"I know who I am" as the True Self—in order for this to occur. But you still insist in claiming the old names. "I am the one who was hurt," "who was damaged," "who is angry," "who doesn't want to deal with anything that he doesn't want to deal with." And then you say, "Well, I guess I am not a Divine Self after all. Look at the mess I'm in."

The mess you claim yourselves in is simply separation from your true identity. Knowing your true identity does not release you from the requirements of your past choices. It is not a free ticket to go murder someone and then remember who you are and assume you are off the hook. You are still claiming the ramifications of past choice, and you will continue to, but the good news is that as you rise above the level of claim that was present when those choices were made, you no longer align to them, and, consequently, even the repercussions will become transformed.

Now when you idealize a future, you decide that all of those things you don't like today will not be there. "I will have a lovely life when the children are out of the house." "I will have a lovely life when I get to retire." "I will have a lovely life when everybody agrees with me and I am in charge of everyone." You will be waiting a very long time for that one. It will not happen.

But what you are truly saying is that you have opportunities here and now to know yourself in the true way that we speak to—through your children, with your job, and with an entire community who doesn't want to agree with you, and perhaps for good reason. The realization of the True Self comes at the cost of the known, and the realization at the cost of the known renders past choices as released because you don't need them anymore. When you no longer need the approval of your community, you are in fact free of it. And because you no longer need the approval, you are no longer serving it out of fear, or seeking to appease or be approved of for being who you think you should be.

The idealization of a future that has the things you don't like excluded may in fact be something that comes, but in most cases you will discover that your relationship to those very things is what has been transformed, and because the relationship to them has changed, because in the higher octave in choice you are not aligning to fear, you release those things by natural or mutual accord that no longer serve anyone.

Now the Christed Self as you must be understood in manifestation. The release of the old paves the way for the new to be in its expression—and by *expression* we mean manifestation—and the alignment that is required for this level of manifestation must come in increments for the field and the form to be able to align to them in full expression. We underline the word *full* expression. We are not speaking in half measures. "I am sort of the Christed Self when I do my good works on Sundays." "I feel like the Christed Self when I read those spiritual books."

This is not about feeling anything. This is simply about the level of octave and manifestation that you realize yourselves through. The Christ as you—not the Christ as the man on the cross, the Christ as you—not the man who walked upon the water and how you would emblazon him with meaning as the one you should emulate, may be well taken if you understand the truth of the message. The Kingdom is here. It has always been here. It is your inheritance. If you want it, you receive it through the realization of the Christ, which is the Divine that is inherent in manifestation as everyone.

The Jesus figure in full realization became the gateway by nature of his expression. So the idealization of the man himself is somewhat confused because what the man realized was beyond the man. And that is the portal for many still to a kind of reunion with Source. But he was come and has come to teach you who you are and what your potential has always been. Each of you here holds the capacity for realization. The density of the plane you exist in has actually transformed to support this. You are no longer slogging through mud to get to the surface of the water and break through to the sky. That was as it was known, and it is not so now.

Now to understand the idea of realization as the Christ, we must take you through a little journey in understanding. If a child remembers his name in the parking lot where he was left, he will be reported by name and sent back to the home that is worried about him. The child is able to say, "I am so-and-so. My mother's name is so-and-so." And he will be returned.

The claim "I am here" is such a name. That is an utterance of the Divine Self in its claim of you, or you as the idealization of the small self that you have come to know yourself as in a lifetime. The Divine as you knows his name, and because he knows his name, he may be reunited with the Source of his being. But if you believe your name is Sam the accountant and Betty the homemaker and Frieda the attorney, you will be stuck in that parking lot for a very long time, and if you are lucky you will be returned to your home or your attorney office only to be left back in that parking lot again.

Now if you understand that the Christed Self knows who he is, who she is, and can claim purview through the announcement "I am here, I am here, I am here," that she can comprehend, as the one who is here, what freedom is, and the only claim that she can make, once she is understood in purview—"I am here"—would be the new claim of freedom. "I am free of what I've been taught, the names I have been called, the edicts placed upon me. I am free of the limitations that the collective has used to inhibit my expression. I am free of the renunciation of my fellows as separate from me. And I am free of the fear that I may be known and come to terms with my true nature as the divine being I have always been."

The idealization of what it means to be in a body must be understood now. You have a body, yes, as a vehicle for experience, and—underline *and*—as a vehicle of your expression. Imagine a body without a soul. It doesn't do much. There is no life to it. It lays in a coffin or upon a slab. But the soul itself is expression, and because the soul is expression at its essence, seeking to align and grow and evolve through every exchange or circumstance that she can claim, she must also understand that expression is her nature. You have a body, it expresses as you in form, and the soul that you exist through is in expression as it.

The separation of form and field is confusing to most of you, but if you can understand that Spirit permeates form and is form itself, you can begin to understand that even that separation is an illusion, and is simply an illustration of density and vibration operating in different octaves. The reclamation of the body in the Divine Self supports the body in becoming the vehicle of the expression of the high octave known as you for the good of the world. Underline *the world*. For the good of the world.

The temptation in a teaching like this is to attempt to misuse it. "He said I was God, they're not very evolved, maybe one day they will be, but until then I am the only God around" supports the small self in a mask of separation that comes at great cost. The moment you think that you are above another, you are below them. Do you hear those words? We are not speaking of status. We are speaking of vibration. And to tell another who he should be by your prescription is in some ways to do exactly that.

The alignment we teach you today in this class, in this text, will be with you well beyond the reading and beyond the lifetime you are embarking on now in this new way. The transformation of the idealization of the small self and its beautiful prison must be understood, and that will be the next chapter of the text we offer you now. Each of you here, each of you engaging with these words, has come to say, "Yes, I may know,

I may be, I may claim, and I may remember who and what I have always been." Period. Period. Period.

(Pause)

Q: The Guides spoke a little bit on your past choices don't go away, but you understand them from the higher octave. Can they speak a little to guilt and exactly what that is and how to get past that?

A: Well, you idealize behavior based upon the cultural mores you've come to, and you forgive yourself only to the degree that you think that you can be forgiven. Guilt is unforgiveness of the self, and shame, we would suggest, colludes with it to keep you from even looking at it. When you decide that who and what you are is meritful outside of what you've claimed in history, you create an opening to a new way of being. If you condemn yourself for who you were, and you carry that forward, you carry yourself forward in a prison. We said "beautiful prisons" when we finished the last teaching, and guilt may be a beautiful prison. You are the occupant. You paint the walls with your guilt and you look at them every day and they confirm what you think of yourself.

The denial of guilt is actually really very simple. It is acceptance. You accept that something happened, that you made a choice. You repair the choice, if you can. You don't continue it. If you wish to be harmful to others and you perpetuate that, you reap the reward of that, and, in fact, you will continue to claim it until the behavior is released. But to recriminate yourself usually does no one any good. Guilt has no effect on positive action. Realization that what you chose was harmful to yourself or another gives you the opportunity to choose anew. Period. Period. Period.

Q: They also spoke about not seeing yourself as above another because in doing so you're actually below, but I'd like to ask a question about this difference in vibration because we're all operating at different octaves, depending on our choices. If you have a family member and you recognize that they're choosing alcoholism and that that affects you . . . I never feel better but I also don't like what they're choosing, and I don't like the way I feel around this person, so it's a tricky road to walk to protect yourself and not feel superior, but also to understand that you're operating at a different level.

A: No, you're not. In fact, you think you are and you're actually above the other only in your own idealization of your own behavior. You are not above them, they are not below you. They are having a different encounter with themselves, and perhaps learning through it, and perhaps giving you the opportunity to learn as well. If you assume that someone is not where they are supposed to be, you have decided for them based upon what you think they should be, or perhaps where or how they should behave based upon your idealization of behavior. Now, if someone is being harmful to themselves, you may offer them help. You may support them or not. You may distance yourself from them, if you wish, if that is the best gift you can give yourself and them. This does not make them wrong. Do you understand this? It doesn't make you wrong, either, but it certainly doesn't make you right. The idealization—"I am the healthy one, they are not so healthy"—has implicit separation inviting itself in the announcement. If you can understand that everyone has come to learn—how they learn their lessons is in some ways decided by them at a higher level—you learn not to judge. You don't have to enable, you don't have to agree, you don't have to drink with them, you don't have to give them money to buy booze. Do you understand this? You can say, "Thank you, no." In some cases, what they are learning through will be what brings them to the light, and no other way would be found. Do you understand this, yes?

Q: The Guides were talking about receiving the Christed Self, and wouldn't it just be perceiving it, wouldn't we already be the Christed Self, but our beliefs are in the way and we're not perceiving it?

A: Yes and no. You are and you can. They are not distinct. You can be the light and still receive the light. Do you understand this? The Christed Self is the truth of your being, but it is not in expression yet in its fullness as who and what you are. To allow that to be is to receive and to align through that reception to its purview. This is the quote. We will use it. "You do not become the Christ. The Christ becomes you." And your realization of it in its expression is its reception as and through you that breaks down or reclaims that which has been placed in fear before the True Self. The expression of the Christ is what transforms the world, and it begins with you. Period. Period. Period.

Q: They spoke a little bit of time about seeing lights and a puff of smoke as if we're seeing in a different octave. Could they explain that a little more?

A: We would like to talk to this because it's about the phenomena that expresses itself when you start unattaching from reality as you have been taught to believe it. Do you understand this? The idealization of form, which we have been teaching for some time—this is a chair because you have been taught it was a chair, when perhaps it could be called something else and perhaps known in a new way— was the beginning of a teaching of re-formation. The idea that everything that has been created can be re-created in a higher way is this teaching. So the fabric of reality is far more fluid than you know, and, as you claim things into form by your agreement to them, you reinforce the history that they have carried. Do you understand this? "My mother said that was a chair and her favorite chair. I know that chair as her favorite chair." And you claim it as such, and you reinforce it in vibration. How you hold anything in witness, or anyone, actually informs the one you see with the level of consciousness you hold. The realization of the Divine in another expressing themselves before you aligns you to them in a higher vibration, and the phenomena he sees is exactly what is happening in the higher realm that the physical eye has not been participating with because he was told it could not be so. Do you understand this? There is much more happening in this room than any of you can see, and the history of this room and all who have been in it are here as well in one way or another, because their consciousness, through witness, impressed themselves upon it. You are participating in history every time you leave your house and you walk upon a road that may have been walked for thousands of years. Do you understand that? The memory of the walk and the pavement and the earth underneath the pavement is still present from all of those who witnessed it. As you confirm history, you make it so. As you confirm the divine nature of all things, you claim that into being as well, and your experience will transform. Do you understand this?

Q: I was struck by the repeated use of the word idealization, *and I wondered if that's part of the new teaching.*

A: How you make things so is idealization, and it is part of this teaching because this is a teaching in how you claim and how you assume. When you assume something to be a certain way, you have idealized something and you expect it to conform to your idea of it. As you realize who and what you are, the small self's idealizations are rendered moot. Do you understand this? The small self's idea of what it means to be happy or successful may mean nothing. They were inherited issues emblemized by you and decided upon with the support of the collective. As you stop idealizing what you should be and how things should look, you can know them in truth, and in truth a lie will not be held. As you align to truth, you may bear witness to the True Self in anyone else—and what a gift *that* is. It sees them beyond prescription and your idealizations of them. "He should not be who I don't want him to be" is an idealization. Do you understand this?

Q: For a person who is empathic, when you are in another person's field and you immediately, automatically, feel what they're feeling and you feel they're in a physical pain or an emotional pain like guilt or sadness or control, the very fact that you are perceiving that level, does that suggest that you are operating on the lower level, and if so, if you are operating only in the higher octave, would you only perceive their True Self empathically?

A: We have two things to say because it is a good question that has not been asked before. You are not confirming the negative by recognizing it. To pretend it's not there would be doing a disservice. "Well, she's a divine being. It doesn't matter that she wants to jump off the roof." That's ridiculous. She is a divine being, and she's so frightened she wants to jump off the roof. The recognition of the Divine will support you in claiming her back, but you don't pretend that the other issue is not present. You don't have to agree with it, which means to move into vibrational accord to it and confirm it for them, which is what they may be wanting. "Tell me it's not worth living." "Well, if you don't want to live, you don't have to" is actually an honest response, "but the idea that you are not worthy of living is preposterous because the Divine as you is here, no matter what you think." You should all understand this. The claim "I know who you are, I know what you are, I know how you serve" is always true because it is claimed at the level of the True Self to the True Self of the one you witness. Do you understand this? You are not making them happy. You are not convincing them to be wrong about what you think they are. You are actually by-passing that and claiming what is always true. At this level the transformation may occur in ways you cannot even imagine. It's the difference between realizing another as capable of change and deciding they cannot change because that's all they are. Period. Period. Period.

Chapter Three

AUTHENTICITY

Day Four (Continued)

Justification of actions taken in prior times must be released now, as well. "I was right to do this or that" in justification appeases the small self and aligns her to a potential where she is not responsible for the action she has taken. To realize the True Self means to be unafraid of what you have done, or has been done to you, because everything can be comprehended as opportunities to learn.

The debasement of the self in some ways comes when you start agreeing to what is not true because it's more convenient, easier for you. And self-justification, we would say, is always the small self seeking to be right. When you release that need, the need to be right and for another to be wrong, you move toward a kind of liberation in your relationships.

You are no longer bartering for who is right. You are no longer playing games of power. You are no longer deciding that your well-being is dependent upon another's behavior. Nobody has to be right, nobody has to be wrong, but everybody has the right to be.

So the True Self, you see, will now begin to support you in accessing information from lifetimes past that may be present in your current life in order to release the patterns that were created and are occupying space in the energetic field, that you have justified and are living with at the cost of the garden that is your soul coming into full bloom. Imagine you have a garden and there are some weeds there. We will give you an example of a weed. "I hate my mother-in-law, she has the right to be, but not around me," "I hate my mother or my sister for what they did," "I will rely upon myself and no one else to get my needs met because nobody's going to take care of me," "I will never be right," "I will always have to assume I'm right so I can fight for what I think is true" would be the ways that the weeds overtake the garden that is seeking to bloom as you.

When you align to the True Self, those things that stand in the way of your growth will make themselves known. They may be from prior times, yes, but you will always have the opportunity in this incarnation to attend to things that were created in past ones. You don't have to go looking for the history. You can assume full well that your attention will be gained by the thing that needs to be seen in order to release it.

If you wish to perpetuate self-justification, you will find yourself in folly, and in the convenience of folly where you forgive only those things that are easy to forgive and comfortable to forgive. Some of you believe that if you are forgiving people for what they have done, you are enabling them to do it again. That is actually not true. To forgive somebody for what they have done is to liberate you. If they came to your house and stole your money, perhaps you don't invite them to tea again. But you do forgive them for what they have chosen to do because you will understand that the ramifications of those choices will be met by them through their learning. Nobody gets off the hook for what they have chosen, but they may reconceive what they have chosen, and learn from it in a higher way.

Now this brings a question to Paul. "Don't we rise above karma when we work at this level?" In fact, you may. You may rise above a past choice and release the need for repercussions. However, we must say, this is not the get out of jail free card. It doesn't work that way. If there is something that you have claimed in fear—and every action you regret may well have been claimed in fear—you may need the opportunity to confront it, in a way, to understand your participation in it, and to release it. What is needed, finally, is your availability to it.

To run away from history is not at all the same thing as releasing history. To deny history is not the same thing as moving beyond it as the source of your creations. Perhaps your mother did beat you, perhaps your husband was unkind, perhaps you were harmed as a child. While we don't deny that these things happened, we do say that how you attend to them decides the life you live with and for you. You are participatory to all of your choices—high, and low, and in between. And incarceration by you, in all cases, is to assume that you are a prisoner of what has been chosen prior.

The alignment to the True Self, who is always free, will begin to break down the walls that you have erected around you in fear or unforgiveness, but your attachment to them being there makes them the beautiful prison we described earlier. You choose your own hells, in some ways, and while these are opportunities to learn, as everything is, you can choose something better if you know you are allowed. The idea of guilt or shame as emboldening you and making you a better person is preposterous. Guilt can be a handy tool—"I feel badly that I did this thing, I will not do it again"—provided the guilt is not about attaching to cultural mores. "I should have curtsied better at the ball. I will not do it again." We would hope you would throw your skirts over your head at the ball and have a wonderful time, regardless of the quality of your curtsey.

Do you understand this? To realize the curtsey doesn't matter is liberating. To feel guilt at not conforming to others' needs is not required and a hindrance to progress. "What might we feel guilty about, then?" he asks. Guilt is not the wrong word, learning might be the better word. "I was angry. I said things in fear. I hurt the woman who cares about me, the man who loves me. I said these things in fear, and now I have the residual actions of that claim before me. I wish to amend the behavior." To amend behavior is to transform behavior. It is not saying you are sorry, it is literally deciding that what was done will not be done because there is no requirement for it. The action of fear is to claim more fear, and angry words, we would suggest, are spoken in fear and then have their own trajectory.

The quality of your lives, in some ways, has a great deal to do with your own authenticity of being and the integrity that you live with, and by *integrity* we mean your availability to truth, regardless of the consequences. "Well, I told a lie. I wish I hadn't said it. I will not do it again." Although the lie that you told may be hurting people in the ramifications of the act you claim, to take accountability for the lie places you in your integrity, regardless of the outcome, and allows you the freedom to act in a new way. If you are busy covering your tracks, you will never learn.

Each of you has been given authority over the world that you live in. By the nature of each encounter that you have, you are aligning to what you think you are or what you truly may be. Imagine, for a moment, that who went to the store is the True Self, who goes to the grocery store is the Divine Self acknowledging everyone she sees and everyone he meets. The small self is there as well. He knows what tea he likes. She knows the fresh lettuce from the poor. She will choose accordingly. But to begin to understand that every choice may be made in a higher alignment, in a new agreement, to choose as the True Self will support great change and in great rapidity.

You wish to protect the choices you like. "I will do it my way. I know it's not the high way, but it's what I want." And you confirm behavior or activity or actions against others because they are convenient to you at the cost of what you know to be true or a higher way of being.

To go into agreement with the True Self is to be in partnership with it, and, as you get comfortable in this partnership, you will actually find that the True Self emerges as the stronger partner, loving you each step of the way. You are not alone or being annihilated. You are being cared for, and, as we have said prior in our teachings, you are assumed by the True Self in your agreement to be as her.

You justify choices and are encouraged to do so, and we would take a moment now to look at how your world asks you to confirm yourself as separate at the cost of others' needs. Every choice that you make, as we said, has ramifications, and you are responsible to the ramifications of them. But if you are instructed to be fearful and you say, "Well, we are being taught to be fearful, so I am not doing anything wrong, I am doing as I am instructed," you give your power to the whole who is basing its act in fear. You do so at the cost of what might be claimed otherwise, and you lose your integrity or your True Self in the process of it.

If you were to be told that the action of the day was to find someone to destroy, would you do it or not? In that language, no. "Why would I do that? I wouldn't destroy anybody." But if we were to tell you that the action of the day was to vilify someone that you are all taught should be vilified, you are more happy than not to go into agreement. "Well, I didn't throw the first stone. It was already thrown. It doesn't really hurt when you throw a pebble, and that's really all I threw." You are in collusion to fear, you are being manipulated, and that pebble may be the last stone that ends a man's life. "But it was just a pebble." It was thrown in fear, in collusion with the whole, and you are accountable to it.

"What would it be like," Paul asks, "if we didn't speak ill of others? We would have nothing to talk about half the day." You find entertainment in it. It has less to do with speaking ill of others on a cosmetic level than the intention behind it. The intention behind it is again self-righteousness, which is the agreement to be the small self. "Well, everybody does it," you say. "We make fun of people all the time. We have our collective villain. It may be another country. It may be someone in politics. We do this every day."

What is the intention behind it? If you can ask yourself this question and become responsible to the action you take in your intent, do as you wish. But your ill talk about anyone else is something that you are accountable to as a choice. This may be an individual or an institution. If you are not bringing peace or light, what are you doing?

"Well, I see injustice. I will speak the truth." If you are speaking in love, you will correct that injustice much more readily than if you are doing it in self-righteousness. "Look at me. See who knows best. Remind me that I am right at the cost of someone else being wrong."

You are tempted every day to make decisions in fear. Only twenty percent of those things are claiming to be fear. The rest are masquerading as something else. Self-righteousness. The need to be safe. The need to be separate. The need to get your needs met through fear or manipulation. You agree to these things, as well, and assume that you don't have responsibility to them.

You are accountable to all of your choices, high, and low, and in-between. Now each time we teach you the mudra of creation, Paul says, "I don't really work with this, but I know it works." We want you all to understand what a mudra is. It is a significant gesture that informs the energetic field and has its own manifestation in the material realm. The mudra of creation is a very simple gesture. If you put your hands before you and call one forth toward you in a circular motion and then the other, as if you are calling things to you in two circles that may not be meeting at the same time, but operating in concurrent ways, you will understand the gesture itself.

Everything is being claimed by you in this way, although this is a metaphor and a mudra itself. Now if you make a high claim—"I am willing to be known as I truly am"—in likelihood you will feel your arms lift to a high level because this is a high claim and a claim of truth. If you let your arms drift to where they are comfortable and make a low claim, "I am going to be the only one here who gets it right," you will probably find that your arms get weighty. You can still claim as the lower self. You have been doing it your whole life. But if you feel the difference in the high and the low, you will understand that a high claim may be made much more easily.

The hands before Paul are continuing to rotate in the mudra of creation, and they are doing so easily because, as he operates as us, he is claiming in a higher way. When his small self comes forth—"Give me what I want" and "I don't think I'm going to get it"—it takes much more effort, but he is used to it, as are you, so you find ways to perpetuate it even if it does not work well for you.

He is interrupting. "You gave us an illustration of a high claim and a low claim. Is there an in-between?" In some ways, yes. Neutrality itself is an in-between claim. "I don't care what happens, let's go to the movie, perhaps we will like it" is a claim that is made significantly in a neutral field. You are not idealizing an outcome, prescribing what should be, and you are not claiming in a high way.

A high claim might be: "I am learning through this encounter. I am realizing the goodness of humanity. I am knowing who I am in this difficult encounter." To claim in this regard calls the high vibration to you, and its manifestation as and through you becomes the field that you operate through.

You are each doing this already in your lives. When you are judging another, you are claiming in low accord. When you are claiming in a high way, you are actually lifting the ones you see, whether or not you know it. You define your reality in most ways by seeing what you see and confirming its merit.

"Look at the tree out the window. That is a beautiful tree. I must be in the country. There is a tree out the window."

"Look at that sky. It looks as if it may rain. There goes my vacation. I didn't prepare for rain."

You are confirming reality by what you see. If you were to begin claiming reality and then confirming the claim, you would have a very different reality. You are affirming what you see, which you are in vibrational accord to, but everything you are in vibrational accord to was claimed by you or others at a high or low level, so you are in octaves of agreement with everything you see.

Imagine what begins to happen, hands held high, the claim being made, one hand over the other in the circular gesture we described, that a new world may be known for the benefit of all. Then the claim is made in agreement to what is not yet seen and then will be known. You confirm the old because you see it and because it's been there, but until you confirm the unknown or unmanifest, all you will get is all you have had.

Some of you decide that the reason you're here is to accept

everything you see, and as you see it, and this is actually accurate. But the question then becomes, "Who sees what she sees and at what level of witness?" Think of one thing in your life that you see every day—a chair, a car, a television set. It matters not. And see it as you've seen it every day, and then invite yourself to see it as the True Self. Does the thing stay the same? Does it begin to transform? Does it have a new idea attached to it, or is it what it has always been?

The True Self will render anything new. So you accept that it's a television, but the True Self receives it in a new way, in a new agreement, to be in relationship to it. So much of what you see was claimed for you that you are in agreement to what you see without even understanding why it was made. There is nothing that was created in form that was not created without intention, and the intention that has made anything into form is present in it now. Every chair bears the memory of the first rock that was ever sat upon for comfort. Every tree bears the memory of the seed that grew it and planted the field of trees thousands of years ago. Every human being still holds the DNA or the memory and idealization of its first ancestor.

We don't make these things wrong, but we do say your confirmation of history is as far as you get in manifestation until you agree that what may be claimed may be made new.

We will continue this teaching later in the day. We will take a pause for Paul.

(Pause)

Some of you decide that this will be the life where you decide that anything can be so, and what this means is the transition from the small self to the True Self has claimed a world that could not be known otherwise. The transition from small to great, or small to true, is a deep passage, and one that is fraught in many ways with trials. But these are the trials that were claimed by the small self and must be reclaimed in a higher way by the True Self as its passage to freedom claims a world anew.

Everything that you can imagine that can be known in fact can be known. There is nothing impossible, finally, that you can claim, because in some reality everything is possible. You have been living a diminished life in many ways, prescribed by what came before you. And what was taught to you as impossible is only impossible in the jurisdiction that the small self has attended to.

When you begin to bypass rules and claims made for you, you often encounter resistance. "Who are you to say such a thing? Such a thing cannot be so." And it may not be so in this dimensional reality, but it is certainly true in potential. Underline this. *In potential* all things are possible. *In potential* all things may be claimed. But unless you attend to anything in its potential, it cannot be realized or known.

"Humanity cannot become the Christ" is a claim of the small self, perhaps the claim of a church, or a heretical claim made by some who would deny the authorities that came before them. The Divine as what you are is not in the least bit a heretical teaching. "All is holy" is the fundamental reasoning to support that claim. "All is holy," including the bodies you've taken. But as the body begins to realign to a higher degree of manifestation, which means resonance in octave, it must announce the new at the cost of the old.

Now the prescription here would be "as within, so without," and as you announce your freedom in vibratory octave, you witness freedom in what is before you. You are always commensurate to the landscape you exist in. The vibratory field you hold is in agreement to everything you see. So as the body begins to adjust and acclimate to the what that it truly is, it begins to lift in resonance and, consequently, begins to resonate in accord with a higher world.

What was not possible in the small self's world may well be possible in the world that the True Self expresses in. You have heard tales of heaven. You think things, they become so. The imagination rules. All things may be known. In some ways, this is parable. In some ways, this is so. But it is an exemplar of manifestation outside of the density of form, which would ask you to disagree with anything that can be known beyond it.

Divine potential is instilled in you at the creation of your soul. As you come into being in your unique way, your divine potential is embedded in the being of your soul, and it asks only one thing—to realize itself as the who and the what that you have always been at this level of agreement. And its assumption of the soul as a being of light, or as an expression of God, is its action, lifetime after lifetime, and then beyond that as well.

The idealization of a finishing line at the end of this journey must briefly be discussed. Perhaps there is one, but we haven't found it yet. Everything is in motion, and the reconciliation to the reality you live in as you progress in form and in field is what you will be attending to through the alignments you are aligning as, with, as a result of this teaching. Each of you decides in a higher way what it means to be the True Self, and in fact none of you truly know until its realization as you has made you new. To be made new is to be realized in a higher way. It does not mean you become enlightened and are participatory to the orbs in the sky and speaking with the grass upon the ground. It may well mean that you are aligning to the most potential you can hold in form in the incarnation you are attending to.

Now for those of you who say, "Well, I want it done now, I don't want to come back, I want to float away tomorrow, and if this book doesn't do it, damn them all"—if you want to say that, you may. But what you are also saying is you don't want to be here, you don't want to learn, you don't want to align to anything that is inconvenient to your idea of what your life should look like. And you idealize a promised land where you never stub your toe, where your bills are paid on time, and no one ever gives you a nasty look. That will not happen.

In the higher octave, as you align to it, you still have a body and a reality to attend to, and if you are given a nasty look, we promise you, you won't care. You know better. You know who you are. Becoming the Divine Self does not mean everybody gets to behave as you want them to, nor does it mean that you will not be learning as you progress. We promise you, you will be.

The passages you go through are informed by many things—what your soul requires to progress through, which is what calls your teachings to you, and what you have aligned to as a group soul or in a collective teaching, either through a country, or a family unit, or perhaps a profession. All of you self-identify in collective ways, be it your sex or your profession or your age group. "Of our generation, we learned this or that," and you claimed it as an opportunity to learn, and if it was wrong information, perhaps you have an opportunity now to move well beyond it. As the collective is attended to, first by individuals, and then by the collective whole, the collective progresses. Do you understand this?

We have said for some time that you are way-showers, that you cut away the underbrush of the paths you walk on with your machetes in order to create the room for those who would come behind you. You lay a path through your progress, through your teachings, through your willingness to disobey the law—and we say this intentionally. Any mandate that would prescribe what can be, and is only allowed to be, you may call a law. And if it is there, imagine, perhaps, that there is a reason for it. "Don't go past the stop sign. You might not like what you see there." What lays beyond the sign may be everything you ever dreamed of, but if you are taught not to bypass the sign on the road, you will never go there.

When you decide that being free means you can claim things that you were not allowed to claim in vibration, that you will not be claimed by that which is not in truth, you move to a new identification as the one who knows who he is. The idealization that we offer you here—"I know who I am in freedom"—is the potential that may be claimed by any and all of you, but in potential first. It's not so in your experiential reality yet, but it is true in your experience as a True Self. We will explain this for you. Because at the true level of the Divine Self you are free, it is always true, and aligning to its announcement claims the being you are in its intention—to be free. And as it realigns you and informs your world, your world is transformed to reflect the truth that you have announced. Then there are no prisons except the ones you build for yourselves. The only dark rooms there are, are the ones you go to rest in. There is no fear, but there is wisdom in its place. It may not be a wise thing to go for a dip in the pool with the alligators rushing around. There is no fear of alligators. It is just not so wise to have a swim with them. Do you understand the difference?

As you grow in wisdom, you become the ambassador of this teaching, not by parroting what we say, but by being the expression of your True Self. We express as we can, as we align to Paul, to the degree that his vibrational field can hold us. But as we work through him, our intention is to realize all of you in the field we hold. So as we lift him to where we live, as far as he can go thus far, he lifts you in manifestation by vibrational accord. The texts themselves are in some ways the medium for this because the vibration we sing at informs the words, and the intention behind the words meets you at your agreement. The agreement we spoke of prior was co-resonance, and you are in resonance with all of your en-counters, so to be in resonance with us and our teaching sim-ply means you have agreed to it in field. And as the form confirms it by aligning to the higher octave of its true expression—"I know what I am," the Divine in form and field—its expression is what claims a new world.

You still think that you do the heavy lifting here. There is no heavy lifting, but there are encounters, trials, perhaps, as your learning progresses. An initiatic path, in many ways, supports you in claiming your learning because you know you've earned it. "Boy, was that something. Boy, did I get the lesson. Give me the next one in a kinder way."

Now you are never punished by your teachings, the things you call to you. The small self may be having a tantrum that he cannot get his way, but your True Self is saying, "Oh, good, maybe the young lad will figure it out this time." You don't have to bang your head against the wall to be known or loved or met in your truth, because you never do.

As we teach you today about authenticity, which is the title of this chapter, we teach you what authenticity truly means: To be as you are in truth, without the requirements that you have inherited for one purpose—to sing the song of truth, which claims you in freedom. If you understand this, the passage we have taken you on sequentially in our texts has been to liberation and embodiment because you cannot have one without the other. You cannot have self-deceit and realization at the same time, and you cannot exist in lower vibration and attend to the higher which seeks to realize as you. As you lift, you lift your world, and then everyone else gets to sing along.

Your authenticity also includes the true being you are that is expressed by you on this plane, your innate abilities, your true concerns. The ability to love and caress and to hold another in a body is a deep gift, and one you must be grateful for. To look upon the stars and to bathe in the sea, to feel the air upon you as the wind blows is a wonderful gift, and the sensual self, the skin and bone self, the one who feels and sees, can agree to the pleasures that may be claimed while in a body on this manifestation or plane of being.

The teaching you receive today is going to serve you in two ways, we suspect. It's going to claim you as the one who may know the potential that may now be claimed, and in acceptance of the aspects of the self that have come in form and are often ignored by you. To be a priest does not mean to be celibate. To be a nun does not mean you marry the invisible only. The realization of the Divine in material form in fact renders the world as your lover in a higher way. But you may still know yourself in form, and express the form, and know it in its humanity, the Divine as you in form. The form itself is holy, and humanity, we would suggest, must then be holy as well.

We don't diminish you, but you diminish yourselves. You believe yourselves to be in separation when you are not, and then you claim your world in that agreement, and say, "Oh, no, I have been forgotten." There is no one ever forgotten. An aspect of them, their True Selves, is as present in them as it can ever be, and their soul may be directing them through experiences they may not choose as a small self that are the requirements for their evolution. So never say, "That poor man, that poor woman." She may have come to learn through the very encounter you pity her for, and the compassion you may show her is the gift she actually brings to you.

We will take a pause in a moment, but before we do, we would like to attune the room and the readers of the text as one:

"On this day I claim that the ones I see before me will be known in union, in fullness, and in resolution to be made manifest at the octave of the True Self and call a world into being. On this day I choose to work with my fellows for the benefit of humanity to be realized as the True Self in song, in expression, in field and form. And as I give permission for this, I say yes to all that may be known, yes to all that may be claimed, as the new potential is made known and realized as and through me. I know who I am in truth. I know what I am in truth. I know how I serve in truth. I am free. I am free. I am free."

Thank you each for your presence. We will stop for a moment. Be still and know. Period. Period. Period.

Day Five

As we ask you questions about your requirements for growth, will you answer them in two ways—what the small self thinks and what the True Self knows? "What will make me happy?" What does the small self say when this inquiry is made? "What will make me happy?" What does the True Self speak when you ask this question?

As you begin to realize the True Self as what you are, your ability to access information in many ways becomes apparent, and will become so as you work with it. Each of you comes with an awareness already that there is more to you than you think. That is the gift of the soul whispering to you as you grow. There is more than you see, there is more that may be known, there is more that may be questioned. As you align to the True Self, your ability to access information not only improves, but it becomes what you know.

So the idea even of questioning—"What would be good for me now?"—diminishes because the information is present already as accessed by you through your alignment. The True Self speaks in different ways. You may have a knowing, or a feeling, or a way of knowing in the body what is asking and what is answered. The True Self speaks to each individual in the ways that she may know, so don't assume it should come in a certain way, because it may not.

We ask you questions, and again we say, what is the answer you receive? "What will make me know what I want? I have spent a lifetime not knowing what I want." When you answer this question as the small self, you may get one answer. When you inquire to the True Self, you may get another. The True Self speaks in ways you will understand, as you can claim it.

Each of you here, each of you encountering these words, is in some ways requesting access to information. You assume that information will be the key to wisdom. Information is not the key to wisdom. Knowing is. And the claim we have offered you many times—"I am in my knowing"—will support you in this request being answered, but it rarely comes through information.

Each of you decides, in your own strange way, what will be the best way to learn. "I will learn through challenge." "I will learn through laughter." "I will learn through difficulty." "I will learn through play." You may learn how to be a good friend through a game of chess. You may learn how to be a good friend through losing all your friends and finding out what the deficit has been. Regardless, you can learn and gain information. But knowledge, we suggest, is what becomes of you when information has been so integrated that there can be no questions.

So idealizing information—"There must be another book to read, a class to attend, there must be something that will tell me what I need to know"—will not always support you in the passage you are seeking. In freedom we teach you that what you may claim is anything that may be known that is in truth and in alignment to your requirements for growth.

Anything can be experienced. If you want to go ride on the back of a whale, you may find a way to do so. Anything may be known. You may find a way to claim this knowing. But what is experienced and known, we would suggest, that is in requirement for growth, for your growth and for your availability to be expressed in a high way, are those things that will be met in agreement in your field, and then in manifestation.

The True Self as you, who would like to speak her name

in agreement to what she was taught—"I know who I am, I know what I am, I know how I serve"—is the one who will claim wisdom. And the charity she offers others is the benefit of the wisdom that she has gained. Please do not mistake wisdom for information. Wisdom comes through experience and alignment, and, really, in no other way. Now, you may meet a wise man who has never gone to school. You may meet a fool with many degrees upon her wall. It really matters not what level of education you have had. It matters greatly your availability to learn, and your availability to learn, we would suggest, will come from your willingness to not know, to be available to ignorance so that you may learn.

Those of you who think you know it all stand at a crossroads with a map you have drawn yourself. Why do you wonder when you stumble into the weeds? Why do you wonder when where you find yourself does not resemble what you think it should? Asking to know supports this, receiving knowing supports this, but the only one who asks to know is the one who accepts that he does not know yet.

Paul is interrupting. "Is this a contradiction? If you ask us to claim 'I am in my knowing,' we are claiming that we do, and now you are saying there is benefit to saying that we don't?"

In fact, it is not a contradiction. The True Self knows, and he is the one who claims "I am in my knowing." The small self does not know. She assumes she knows. The map that she carries, once again, was created through inherited idealizations, information, strategies for what you perceive as success and have little bearing in truth. The True Self knows. The small self thinks.

As the True Self begins to align as you, you may ask her questions. "What is the next right act?" "What is the best thing I can do?" "What do I truly need to learn through this encounter that is challenging?" Now, you are not playing games with information. This is not the equivalent of putting bait on a hook and hoping that the fish of knowing bites and you can say, "Oh, wonderful. It actually works. I put the bait on the hook, and now I know." The process of knowing is a little bit different. It actually has to do with acquiescence and availability to claim what has not been claimed yet.

If for some reason you don't know, there is probably a very good reason, and accessing knowing in a higher octave must require that you bypass the thinking that you have substituted for knowing for many, many years. "I know what to pack in my child's lunch," you say, "because I read it in a magazine." That same magazine told you very differently twenty years ago, and twenty years before that it was also a different meal. You are not in your knowing. You are in inherited information and you are doing your best to grasp what you assume to be truth, given the dictates of the day you live in, the day or the year or the time.

The qualifications for being in your knowing are very rich. The soil is already present as you, the being that you are is the one who must know, and accessing the True Self is simply claiming the soil. The richness of your being is accessible to you and contains the requirement for what you know and will ask and will receive in response. The change you undergo is a rather simple one. You stop becoming reliant upon history as the basis for your acts. You stop requiring yourself to imitate the person next to you who looks a certain way, or acts a certain way, or seems to have the answers. You actually bypass the collective information that has been present to claim something higher.

You really cannot claim the higher and the lower at the same time. Now the lower has its place. It's quite wonderful that you pack your child's lunch and that you do the best job you can. But the True Self must know what the requirements are for the child beyond what has been prescripted. This is not about making you psychic. This is not about making you sorcerers who can conjure in wisdom any answer they require. It is about accessing your own knowing at a level of achievement that you can know and be in response to.

The decisions you make from faulty information are with you every day. "Well, it looked like the right house to buy. The real estate agent said it would last forever." The True

Self that you are must realize what is true in the face of what is being spoken.

Now some of you decide that your individual self is your barometer for truth, and while this is not necessarily wrong, you actually confuse yourselves. "Well, I went to see that man, but it didn't feel right. I trust my knowing." Even your feeling senses are being informed by information. You didn't like how he looked, the books you saw upon his shelves, what your best friend said about him, and you carry that information with you as you claim your knowing. What you are truly claiming is "I know that I was confused or was unsure of who this man was, based upon what my friend said, how he appeared, and the books he had on his walls." Your intuitive self perhaps was speaking to you but was still accessing data to prove a point.

Some of you feel that your knowing is your opinion, and you must look at this carefully. "That is not the man for you," says the woman who decides that she knows what is best for her child. "That is not the man for you. I know it." That is not the man she would prefer her daughter marry, and her opinion is being claimed in a way that would mask her fear of what could happen to her daughter if she marries a man she does not approve of.

The escalation of vibration for each of you will summon knowing to you, as a field does. Now, the field that you hold can pose a question. "What do I require to learn next?" And you can ask the question in the field, and then assume that the response will come through your encounters, through the manifest world, through the ideas you find bubbling up in response to the question. The claim "I am here, I am here, I am here," which is the claim of the True Self in its purview, is of great help here. When you begin to operate with that claim, the True Self announcing its purview, you go into agreement with the requirements of the True Self, and that includes what you need to know.

Imagine that you are planning a party. You want everybody to be happy. You want each guest to be very pleased. Where do you put the place mats? Where do you put the flowers? Where do you put the drinks? "Will so-and-so speak to each other if I put them beside each other?" You question these things and you assume what should be, and as you act in your suppositions, once again you do the best you can. As you go into alignment with the True Self—"I am here, I am here, I am here"—you begin to operate in agreement to know, because the True Self knows and the small self supposes and thinks.

Paul is getting in the way. "But this is *The Book of Freedom*. Is this in the book? Is this a teaching on freedom? What are we to do with this information?" This is in the book, and it is a teaching in freedom because, unless you are in your knowing, you will be supposing. And if you are supposing, you are entrenching yourself in the data that you assume you must need to act upon. As you go to knowing, it becomes like breathing. You know what you need to know, you know where you stand, you know what will make you happy, and the agreements are made. But you are still so busy listening to the small self's voice that you ignore the True Self that is as available to you.

You will ask yourself a question now. "Where is my growth needed? What area of my life is my growth needed?" And see what the response is that you get as you ask the True Self to become the teacher. "How do I learn this?" is the next question you ask, and you receive an answer. Let yourself receive. Don't assume it's right or wrong. Allow the answer from the True Self to come forth.

Now the last question, we would say, is "Am I who I say I am?" And who answers the question will give you the answer of what voice you are listening to. The True Self knows who she is. There is no question. The small self assumes and thinks, looks beyond her for the mirrors of her worthiness or her value, seeks to decide dependent upon what the person beside her has just done. Do you understand this teaching?

As we continue in this chapter, we will claim you anew as the one who may know, and we will say these words on your behalf:

"On this day we claim that each one who attends to these words is in reception of their own truth as the one who may know. And in their claim—"I am here, I am here, I am here"—they may access their knowing as the one in truth, who is not deceived by the mandates that the small self would gift her with. As I align to truth, I know. As you align to truth, you know. And the claim that you make for each one you meet is the claim of truth. I know who you are in truth. I know what you are in truth. I know how you serve in truth. I am in my knowing. Word I am Word."

Thank you each for your presence. We will take a pause for Paul. Period. Period. Period.

(Pause)

We would like to say a few things about where they think they are on their path, in their lives, on these journeys that they have chosen.

The first thing you must understand is that you can only be where you are. This moment in time is the perfect place and the only place for you to learn through. Everything is chosen in a certain way by the requirements of your soul. And it is your soul, we would suggest, that gave you an encounter with us, and the opportunities that arise from this are the ones that you require individually and collectively to learn through and evolve with. Your evolution, we suggest, as a species is actually predicated upon the awakening of those of you who will lift the plane through intention and agreement to what it may be known as in a new way.

We have taught you the Kingdom, the awareness of the presence of the Divine in all things, and it is here now, has always been, will and only can be here now, as you are, but your alignment to it has been inhibited by the vibration of fear and collective agreements in separation. The individual, once she begins to understand that she is free, free of the collective rule, free of the established pattern, free of the decisions made for her and by her in agreement to the collective, shifts the frequency that she inhabits. In some ways, the vortex that you become aligns you to the requirements of the realization of freedom, which is in some ways the key to the Kingdom.

When you know you are free, you know everybody else is as well, and you unlock the doors, the cellars, the prisons that others have existed in, less through action, but by being. The field that you hold begins to operate in support of all by nature of your being. This does not mean you are not living a life, or having your employment, or learning your lessons. It simply means that the echo of your vibration in field and form, the expression of it as echo or tone, informs the world and becomes catalytic for the awakening of others.

To be awakened is to come to terms with the reality that has existed beyond you. It does not mean you become the bright light of the world, but you become a bright light along with all of your fellows. And the shift on this plane that will then occur will be a shift in climate and agreement to climate. Now we are not speaking to climate as weather, but environment, and the environment you live in is actually informed by vibration and collective issuance about what you think should be there. Underline the word *think*. The habituation of humanity on a dense plane has been made by humanity. The field that you hold collectively, in collective agreement, has been made by you, one and all.

The Divine Self, who is as you announcing herself as free, claims a broadcast in this dense field, and those who abide in it will begin to awaken to the call. Now it doesn't mean that you demonstrate yourself as free. "I will break all the rules. I will wear no clothing. I will wear a bell on my head and everywhere I go I will ring my bell and people will sure know I am there." You can, if you wish, but you *are* the bell ringing, and you *are* naked in field, you *are* lifted to be seen in an enlightened way.

The Divine as what you are in manifestation as you operates on multiple levels. You have a life here that you take care of, but you are also in issuance, by nature of being and relevance, to the call of the time. You are ringing a bell. "I am free, I am free, I am free." But what this bell sings, as much as your name, is the name of all of those you encounter. "You are free, you are free, you are free." You are the town crier, yes, wakening people from their slumber by nature of your being.

Each exchange you have with a fellow is an invitation to know who they are in their liberation. If you take the focus off of yourselves, even for a day, and invite everybody you meet to truly be seen by you, and you claim them in their freedom, they will be lifted by this encounter even if the only words you utter are, "Hello, how was your day?" The truth of your being in vibration informs every encounter.

The delineation that you make between small and true will begin to diminish as the true overtakes the small. Then you just become who you are in your expression. Your expression: "I know how I serve." Your service is your expression, the Divine as you in form and field and being, the Divine as what you are manifest here for the benefit of your fellows, those you will meet and may never meet.

The issuance of the True Self in the field you hold is catalytic to everything that it encounters. You must understand this. You are radios, you are playing a broadcast. The broadcast is not heard by mortal ears, but experienced in the field as an awakened self. Here's a song that awakens her from her slumber. The vibration you hold is the issuance, and the claim you make is the song. The field you hold is the echo of the essence of the True Self informing all it encounters. When it is catalytic, it has effect. The broadcast you hold has effect upon all that it encounters.

Today, make a promise, if you wish, to stand before someone, anyone, and know who they are without telling them what you're doing. Claim it for them silently, and then feel the response you get from making the claim for them. "I know who you are in truth. I know what you are in truth. I know how you serve in truth. You are free. You are free. You are free." You will receive the residual effect of the co-resonant act.

Understand this. Everything you claim you are in relationship to at the level of vibration or accord you are attending to it in. When you claim something as awful, you receive the residual effect of that awfulness. You are in exchange. When you claim something as holy, the holiness that is implicit in what you see blesses you back.

"Is that why people pray over their food?" he asks us. Well, the effect of praying over your food is the intention to realize the holiness that you are taking in to your own body, so that's a perfect example. But it can be done with a cloud in the sky or a stranger that you meet on a path. "All is holy, as am I."

The trust that you require to engage on this journey with us is the trust in the self, the True Self, you see, who would lead you well with your permission. The free will that you have been given is utilized in its highest way when it is allowed to be received by the Divine. "Take my will. Use me well. Let me be in service." These are claims you may make. But the Divine as what you are, in alignment in will, will express with you. Do you understand that? Express with you. As you sing your song in your ordinary life, the job you go to, the meal you make, the drive to work, whatever it is, you are still singing in the higher octave, and all you encounter is in benefit from this.

Paul is interrupting. "Can we know this? You speak of knowing. This sounds extraordinary. How do we know this?"

When you decide to do this work, you are actually being prepared, with our intention, to serve, know it or not. That is part of the agreement we gift you with to support you in the awakening and realization and expression of the True Self. So you require knowing in your expression and a tangible experience of the Divine Self to know that this is so. We will offer you this as we can.

Wherever you are now, wherever you hear these words, or read these words, take a moment in silence and we will sing your song for you. And as we break through the density of the fields you have held, as we lift you to our level of agreement, we say these words to you one and all: "You are free, you are free, you are free." And as you allow this to be known, allow the field that you hold to sing back in echo, "I am free, I am free, I am free."

And in union we do this, in participation with you where you sit or stand or lay. Wherever you be and however you be in this perfect moment we share, at this perfect juncture in your lives, we say, "Yes, you are here," and know that you are free. Period. Period. Period.

Stop now, please. This is in the text, yes.

Chapter Four

PREPARING FOR
THE KINGDOM

Day Five (Continued)

Some of you decide in advance that this will be the lifetime where you remember who you are. Let's talk about remembering only for a moment. Your ideas of who you are, in most cases, were claimed in this lifetime through appropriation and agreement to your surroundings, your culture, those things you see that would define you that you attend to on a daily basis. When you go beyond this lifetime to the well that is always there, you can access truth that is not limited by the life that you live. The truth of your being extends well beyond a lifetime, and well before, as well.

Imagine, for a moment, that you had access to information that would support you in claiming the Divine Self in a new authority. This is a very simple idea. If there were a memory that you could access of your divine heritage that did not key to a memory of this lifetime that is fraught with the issues that you have attended to throughout your life, you could claim an idea and a remembrance and a solidity to the claim "I know who I am."

If you understand that when you think of who you are—underline *think*—of the small self, the database that you are accessing was created in this life. "I remember that year at the beach. I remember when I dated that person, my first day at school, how my father held me, what my mother said I was." So the "I" self, in many ways, has been decided for you through these experiences, which is why you are so challenged at times by claiming the Divine, who exists beyond these things, exists before, exists after, always exists, we will suggest, in one form or another.

To support you in this memory, we must go to a time without time, and we want you to imagine, for a moment, that you are lifting from your chair—in the body you hold, if you wish, or without the body, if you wish—to a time without time, to a place that does not exist with a clock handy or a calendar present to tell you who you should be. The Divine Self as you extends to this place very comfortably because the Divine Self exists without time. He is timeless, she is free of time, although she knows herself in time, through you, to support you in your requirements of realization of her essence.

The Divine exists outside of time, and an aspect of you now has lifted from your chair to be at this timeless place where you may now access information that may be required by you to support the memory and coherence of the true claim "I am here." Once you understand that truth is truth, wherever you are and whenever you imagine yourself to be, you will not be grabbing at straws, clawing at the embankment, trying to climb out of the well that does not cohere to where you think you should be. The Divine is present now in this timeless place for you to know yourself in.

Now as you float here in this timeless place, imagine that you are being attended to by those of us who have come to support you in your awareness of the divine essence of yourself, and we will invite you now to ask us for a memory, a physical memory, an image, an idea, anything that will show you your True Self that exists outside of time, the I Am, the True Self that is you. The self that we speak to in this moment will be the True Self, and we are requesting on behalf of all of you that you be met by that aspect, the eternal self, in a way that you can claim from here on in as your mentor, your Divine Self. The alignment that he brings you, she brings you, can and will bring you joy in this great meeting of the eternal and the temporal.

The small self is now going to say, if you are willing to say it with her, "I am willing to know myself outside of what I think I am," and now agree to the memory and the attendance of us that will show you who you are. Be received by your own True Self. Be received by the memory of her, her inception, his claim, his face, his love, the Divine Self in whatever form he wishes to express as, as who you are.

> "I allow the Divine Self to give me the memory I require to know myself in fullness toward my realization of who and what I am in perfect manifestation. I am here. I am here. I am here."

Once you attend to the language we use in realization, the claims we make for you that you speak on our behalf for your own well-being are known by you in a much deeper way. The claim "I am here," the Divine Self in purview, may be uttered in a castaway fashion. It may be uttered in truth. When it is uttered in realization, it becomes the memory that will solve all your problems, because all your problems, we suggest, are the result of misidentification with who and what you think you are. The I Am self, the one who is here, the one who is free, the one who knows her name, has come as you to bring forth the value of her expression, his essence, to support a world in change.

Now we would like you to imagine that this aspect of you, the True Self as you, is in fact boundless. He has no edges, she holds no limitations, and her awareness of herself in a small way is no more challenging to her than her awareness of herself in a vast way. Imagine that the light you are, the Divine Self that you are, is now expanding and increasing in value and vibration. As you expand, everything that you encounter and is known by you is known by you in truth. You are the one who is free and, consequently, has the right to announce herself before all she sees to claim the liberation that is inherent in the divinity of all matter.

The Divine as you expands beyond this space you sit in, beyond the walls of the space you sit in, beyond the county lines, across the rivers, across the continent, across the oceans, around the globe, and beyond that as well. Imagine that the being that you are in vibration is holding itself in love, and all that it includes in its vibration is facing the same liberation that you are claiming for yourself. Now you may say these words to all that you encounter, and do so silently, please:

"On this day I choose to be remembered as my True Self in service to the world before me. On this day I choose to give permission to my Divine Self to be in expansion and in song for the awakening of humanity to claim itself in unity with its Source. As I say yes, I say yes to all I encounter, yes to all I see, yes to all that may be known, yes to all that may be claimed in the highest octave I am available to be in broadcast with. I know who I am in truth. I know what I am in truth. I know how I serve in truth. I am free. I am free. I am free."

Feel this, yes. Now you have claimed a world in newness by your issuance. You have moved out of linear time to the place where you are timeless. You have remembered the essence of your being and you have announced her, you have announced him, you have announced it, if you wish—"I am here"— and, in this claim of freedom, you have claimed liberation for all that you will encounter. The vibratory field that you hold, which holds this information in like accord, claims all it sees, all it witnesses, all it encounters, in the same field. And your agreement to do this has supported the world in change.

When we say these words now, we say them in love: Stop pretending you are not who you are. Stop lying to yourselves and saying you are your pain, you are your suffering, you are your fear. Stop saying to yourself that you have no right to claim the Kingdom. That is a claim of fear. We are saying this for you now, wherever you are, whoever you are, whatever you think you have done or could be accused of. Whatever you have named yourself as in limitation, we say this to you. We will not agree to you anymore at the level of fear. We will not support you anymore in acquiring more fear. We will not say yes to it. And we say this in love. We know who you are, even when you deny it, and we will not agree to the shame, the blistering fear, the condemnation of your fellows that humanity has wrought, because the price you pay for this is far too great. You are deeply loved. The one you would find the most horrible on this plane is deeply loved. We suggest this to you. The Divine as you is here, is here, is here, and must be sung.

Now the alignment is here for this to occur. This is reason to rejoice. The alignment is present for this to be claimed. This is reason for cheer. The manifestations of fear that you may see playing out before you can still be realigned in the truth of your being, and in your willingness to serve in the octave of truth and freedom.

As we say this for you now, we say a prayer with you. We claim that all mankind may know love. We claim that each being on this plane may become an emissary of peace, so that you may put down your swords and embrace your brothers and sisters in the realization that all is holy, all is holy, all is holy, as are you. Period. Period. Period. Period. Period. Stop now, please.

In the text. New chapter. Please call it "Preparing for the Kingdom." Period.

(Pause)

Now when you listen to us, you presuppose several things. You presuppose that your needs will be met in one way or another. You presuppose that we know what we are speaking about. And you presuppose that there will be benefit to attending to these words.

The suppositions you make about us and our relationship to you in some ways decide for you what this experience will be. This is an experience of communion, of sorts, with an aspect of the Divine that is coming in form and speaking words for the benefit of those who attend to them, the Divine in form. We come in form through Paul to teach you that your form is also the vibration of the Christed Self, once the Christ assumes the form it has taken.

The Christ as you has been this teaching since the beginning, although many of you dislike the term *Christ* because it's been fraught with history and meaning, which has impaired the truth of it. The vibration of the Christ, or the Divine in manifestation, has been the truth of this teaching since we first uttered the words "I am the Word."

Now we know who we are, and because we know, we know who you are as well. We are not babying you. We are claiming you as the adults in spiritual growth that in fact you always are when you stop lying to yourselves about the what that you are. The misinformation that you have been encoded with through cultural appropriation, historical data, is what has stood in the way of realization. The belief that you need permission from a father, a sage, a teacher, a priest, or absolution for your sins to ascend in Christ as the Divine Self has been the issue that has hampered your development.

You do need absolution, but it cannot come from a man. You cannot know the Divine without being willing to be known. Do you understand this? And to be known also requires you to expose yourself to the Divine to be rendered new. The idealization of sin as unpardonable, what it means to be sinful, how the names have been used against others, must be re-understood. To be exposed to the Divine, to say, "Here I am, all aspects of me, the fear I have used against myself and others, the shame of the body, or the fear of failure, the damnation of my fellows that I have engaged in"— all of these things must be revealed to be lifted.

Now they don't exist at the level of the True Self. They are the weeds in the garden that need to be pruned for the true flower of your soul, which is the Christ within, to envelop the garden, which is your soul. And the pruning takes place when you give permission and you say, "Yes, here I am." The agreement to be seen as you truly are, not hiding the self, not hiding in shadow, is the idea that is behind confession.

The idea that what is exposed to the light will be claimed by the light brings absolution, yes. But the idea that there is penance attached is in some ways idolatry. The idea that offering yourself to the Divine, but the Divine would throw you back as unworthy, must be seen as a creation of fear. And that any human being could be rejected by the Divine because of what he has done or believes he has done must be seen as what it is, a doctrine in fear.

The Divine as what you are must be met by the truth of your being, and the truth will make you free. To deny your fear or your shame, to hide under a bush, if you wish, so that your light will not be seen, will heal no one, will bring no joy. The claim we make for you—"We know who you are in truth"—is in itself a claim of liberation. We know who you are without the fear, without the shame, without the condemnation of yourself and fellows. But unless you listen to it and understand that these things must also be offered by you to be assumed by the Divine, the garden will not be cleared.

"How is this done?" you may ask. There are many ways it can be done. There is not one path to this idea of being reclaimed at the cost of the old, and this is in fact one of the things we mean when we suggest that the new self comes forth at the cost of the old. If you wish to offer yourself to the Divine in fullness, every aspect of you, you must be met with the opportunity to transform. If you wish to undergo a passage or a discipline that claims these things with you, there is nothing wrong with that, either. The simple teaching here is that the Divine as you will be realized once she is allowed to weed the garden, but she will not take from you what you protect and hide.

Now if you wish, take a few moments and decide the things that you have kept from the light—the shames, the angers, the requirements of others to be who you think they should be, the self that has been fearful and bound others in fear. What are the aspects of the self that are the weeds in the garden that is you? And, if you are willing, we would like to release you from the very things that you have protected yourself from. "If nobody sees the weeds in the garden, they will not know that I am shameful, that I did this thing, that I cursed that woman, that I bound myself in fear to a relationship without love"—whatever the weeds may be. If we are allowed to see them, if you are willing to be shown as what you are, weeds intact, the pruning may begin.

Now we use the word *pruning* only for illustration. In fact, what happens in resolve is that the Divine as you in its manifestation will claim you in liberation with the claim we have offered you: "I am free, I am free, I am free." Imagine, if you wish, that the Divine Self as the soul, blooming within the soul, is seeking to eradicate the restrictions of the weeds that have coiled around it and stopped it from its full bloom. Imagine that the Divine Self is the one who says yes in its unbound way: "I am free, I am free, I am free."

Now we will say this for Paul, who always has concerns.

This is not magical thinking. The claim "I am free" is operating in vibration. The attunement has been given to you to align to freedom through our witness and/or our claim for you, and each of you who has said the words, wherever you have read them, or seen the man before you, who speaks them, will understand that in co-resonance the attunement to freedom has been claimed for and with you. There is no magic here at all. There is co-resonance and agreement, and then manifestation must follow.

So once again we invite you to look around your garden, see what has sprung from the soil that would seek to diminish you. Have you watered the weeds? Have you rolled around in the dirt and embraced the things that give you the most pain? Many of you do. You find solace in suffering. You find power in anger. You find ways to debase others so that you may feel superior and therefore worthy. These are the things that must be attended to.

Now we will say these words with you wherever you may hear them. And when we say them, we will encourage you to say yes, in silence, to the claims that are made on your behalf:

"On this day I choose to be liberated from all of the obstructions that I have used to deny my true name. I am free. I am free. I am free. And in this claim of truth, I give permission to my Divine Self to amplify in fullness for the perfect eradication of those energies that would seek to suppress my Divine Self from its manifestation and expression in truth. As I say these words, I give the expression of the Divine, which is in love, the perfect opportunity to encompass all of the obstructions and realize itself at the cost of what has been claimed in fear (or in anger, or in greed, or in shame, or in gluttony, or whatever word or label you wish to use to codify the idea of separation)."

You have heard of seven deadly sins. You may list them, if you wish. They are all ideas of separation and nothing more. We sing your song with you now. We see the ones before us as free, as in liberation, and in a new claim of truth. You are free. You are free. You are free. Allow the light that you are to bloom you, to emblazon you, to claim you in its ferocity and in its great love.

Now the song has sung, the day is ending, this teaching is finishing for the day, and we sing our song in gratitude for those of you who attend to us. We are humbled by your willingness to release that which is no longer needed for your realization. We will work with you, as well, as you step up to be seen, to be revealed, in your perfect way. Period. Period. Period. Stop now, please.

Day Six

We ask you each for willingness today, and willingness is required, to release the ideas you have held as sacred about who and what you are. The Divine as what you are is the only true thing that you can claim as an eternal self. The other ideas that you hold sacred are all passing, will be transformed one day or another, so your willingness today to allow, to allow, to allow the release of the profane, that which is not sacred, or idealized as sacred, when in fact it is not, must become the truth of the action of the morning. This is a teaching of release and acceptance at the same time.

There are things that you believe that you cannot live without. There are ideas you hold about yourself that you will not release because you believe, if they are released, you will be trampled upon. You will be seen as inferior. You will be lost to the crowd without the identity that you have attached to.

The reason we do this work with you is not to make you wrong in these attachments. Anything that you have claimed in this way, you believed you needed and most likely did—for your own survival, your own sense of well-being. So please do not think we are making you wrong. We are liberating you, and that's a very different thing.

You idealize, in some ways, the very things you wish would go. You claim things over and over and over that you wish would not be there. You are participatory, not only to your own life, but to the world you live in, and your agreement to be in it has required you in many ways to design a world that would allow you to live in it. The small self's world, if we could say it, is in some ways a prison, in some ways a classroom, in some ways a glorious creation. We don't make that wrong, either. But the idea of liberation from the known, and liberation from those idols that you have attached great meaning to, is the work of the day.

Here we go. If you will say this after us very softly, barely a whisper, as Paul likes to say:

"On this day I present those aspects of the self that require liberation, that I have held as sacred, that I have used to keep myself safe or important or free of fear. On this day I allow myself the privilege of moving beyond the known and realigned to a level of accord where these are no longer requirements for my being. And as I agree to this, I give permission to my entire being to be recalibrated in the higher octave to a level where these things no longer abide. I choose this of my own free will in the awareness that my claim of freedom, my liberation, will be of benefit to me and all that I encounter. I give thanks for this. And as I say yes, I acknowledge the Source of all things, who will hold me in its light to be known anew. I know who I am in truth. I know what I am in truth. I know how I serve in truth. I am free. I am free. I am free."

Feel this, yes. Allow the wind to blow through you. Allow the claims you have made to be known. Allow the choice you have made to be respected. Allow the decision to be made known in form, and field and, yes, expression. The wind is blowing through Paul, now. He is understanding it as a release. What he is releasing is in his design for who he should be, and those agreements that he expected to manifest that are unmanifest will be releasing so that the manifest self can express itself without the disfigurement of the false self's requirement.

We ask you each this: If you could transform one thing in your life, one issue, one problem, if you would like to claim it as such, what might it be? And then you say these words:

"I am free of this thing I have claimed in fear. I am free of this thing that I have used to keep myself separate from my Source. I am free of the requirements it gave me to live in its accord, and as I say yes, I say these words, I am free, I am free, I am free."

Feel this, yes? Let the wind blow through you. Let the light come through you. Let the claim be written in the field you hold. Let it be sung in a resounding yes that you are in freedom, and how can you not be when you know who and what you are?

(Pause)

Now the thought of each of you coming into your own frightens you. You decide yourselves what your experience should be as a Divine Self. "I must walk on water. I must be wise all day long." And because you assume, with some certainty, that it will not be that, you condition yourselves to decide how far you can go.

"I will be my Divine Self if I am present in an acceptable way."

"I will be my Divine Self as long as I am getting my needs met in the physical realm in the ways that I should."

"I will be the Divine Self for you, in some ways, but not in private. That's too hard. I cannot be the True Self in my own company."

The decisions you make about what it means to be realized, and what you bring to that in ideology, in most cases serve to mask the conditioning that would come if you allowed yourself in full expression. The True Self in full expression is something that you can't fathom, so there is every reason why you decide what it should look like, attempt to frame it by an idea or inherited structure that you can attend to with some sense of comfort.

Imagine, if you wish, that there was a light that was bright, but you only assumed there could be so much brightness, you only assumed that the bulb itself could hold a certain wattage. You will never find out what the bulb can hold unless you turn the wattage up. Now what is illumined by that bulb, that small bulb in full realization, may be an entire world, but you have decided that your little self, in its most emblazoned light, may light up the street corner you sit on, and perhaps no more.

The True Self seeks liberation, and that is the claim "I am free, I am free, I am free." The True Self seeks liberation in its expression, and its magnitude will be its own claim. If you stop prohibiting manifestation beyond what you have thought can be so, each one of you by nature of being can claim a new world into being. Each one of you by name—"I am free, I am free, I am free"—will claim a world into being where the True Self is operating outside of the box that it has been placed in by your need to stay small, by the institutions you've attended to, or the books you've read thus far that say this is all about being happy, getting your needs met, having a better life, and then going back to sleep.

To become awakened is to become realized, and the realized being that you are will seek expression in all avenues, not just the polite ones, not just the ones you assume should be there. By the claim "I am free," you are actually giving permission to reclaim the self outside of the promises that were made by you about what you can manifest, and how you can manifest, and how you can know a world. You are free from prescription, you are free from others' decisions, but beyond that the True Self is free to create anew.

Now this is a new idea for you because you understand manifestation to be the product of thought. "I thought this thing. I claimed it into manifestation or vibrational accord." You still assume that the Divine Self in purview will operate that same way. But it will work well beyond that in its expression. If you can imagine that there is an aspect of you that knows all of your requirements for deliverance from the small self, that knows the requirements to claim the world into being where she can know herself in the higher octave she sings at, that can be party to a revolution in transformation on this plane through the re-identification of the manifest world in its true identity of divine seed and flower, the

Christ Self or the True Self will do what it requires. And you still think that you as the small self, assuming yourself to be the Christ or the Divine Self, has to figure it all out.

That is no longer the case. The alignment we bring you now to the Divine Self has a requirement—that you give permission to the will itself to go into accord with the vibration of truth, and then the vibration of liberation. The will itself, the aspect of you that knows what it needs, or assumes it knows what it needs, must be met and responded to by the True Self for integration to occur. "Thy will, not mine, be done" has been a claim you have heard. And it is a true claim, but the "not mine" actually signifies that the small self's will is now being assumed by the Divine Self and not operating in opposition to it. "I won't get my way, thy will be done, I can't fix it anymore" is how you have known surrender. But the braiding of the will, the small and the true, and the assumption of the will by the Divine Self is what claims will in expression without the kind of thinking that the small self has used to define its requirements in codified ways.

Now when you are willing to know yourself in a higher way—"I know who I am in truth"—you claim a possibility that the aspect of you that knows, the True Self that knows, will support this acclimation of the will to its true source. In some ways, what you are doing in offering the will to be braided and then assumed by the Divine is entering into an agreement that you are being supported by the Divine, and you are not being left behind. The fear that you encounter in this act of surrendering will is that you assume that you will not get what you want, and even your idea of enlightenment, which you demand, will not play out as the small self assumes it should.

The True Self is the one who expresses and supports the requirements of the life lived, and the Divine Self, in its agreement to be, manifests what is required for the self to evolve through. Imagine, for a moment, that you had a map that would reveal each step as it was meant to be known. That is the map you carry as the True Self. Each step will be met by you in an agreement to be manifest, and manifest in truth. When you assume that the map you carry has frightening possibilities—too many tangents, too many roads, too much debris blocking the pathways of some—you seek to stay where you are or seek to confirm a choice by asking everybody else, "Which way should I go? What is the right path for me?" The True Self guarantees that each step will be made and revealed as it is required.

Now some of you don't like this. "But I have grand ideas for my future, who I should be and what I should become. What happens to my five-year plan if I only know the next step? I would suggest," says the small self, "I keep my five-year plan and ignore the next step if it doesn't confirm where

I think I am supposed to go." That is the way you decide to sit on the sidelines and assume that your life will be met by you in the ways you think it should. You hold the will, you hold the guarantee that the small self requires that things will happen as he or she thinks they should at the cost of what would be offered to you, one step at a time.

Now when we speak of a step, we speak of an act, or a change, or a movement forward. And as we suggested, the True Self will offer you this much as you can claim it, and by *claim* we mean be in vibrational accord to. Each step is manifest, and then the next step is laid. You may have this passage come quickly or slowly. It really matters not. All that truly matters is that you have the trust that, through the braiding of the will, each step will be made known to you as it needs to appear for your benefit and for realization to occur. Again, once we say realization and knowing are the same thing, we confirm for you that you will know and realize what this requirement is as you take that step.

You say you want great things, but your idea of a great thing is still informed by the small self in his ambition to be known by the world as he assumes he should be seen. Even those of you who are striving for enlightenment are operating in the small self, because the small self's decision of what enlightenment is may be driving you. The alignment as the True Self through an act of will, and with the agreement to operate in accord to will at a higher level, is what transforms this. And how you know it is so is that you begin to operate sequentially in an awareness of your requirements for growth, and that the path unfolds in ways you can comprehend. The idea that you are no longer listening to the self and seeking advice elsewhere is relinquished because the True Self becomes what you attend to in will and in agreement.

So he has a question. "But what if I want something and I want someone, or I want something to be made so and it's important to me? What do I do with desire, and is it in conflict with the will, as you speak to will?"

It is not necessarily in conflict, but the bullying to get it and the demand to have it is always the small self seeking to get what it thinks it should have. If you require a relationship with another to learn through, and it is supported by you in vibrational accord—which means you can operate at a place of reception for the thing that you require—you can well accept that it may be made so in form as it's required. Underline *as it's required*. *As it's required* means that it is not the small self's agenda for development, but the True Self, who is saying, "Yes, what a wonderful opportunity for realization."

Everything on this plane may be experienced or known. We are not speaking to you about limitation. In fact, the liberation of the True Self, and the alignment of the will, will claim for you things far more greater, than the small self can assume, for the simple reason that the True Self is knowing its worth and can receive these things. If you understand that the basis for one of our texts was humanity's inability to conceive of itself as worthy of divinity, you can understand that as that divinity is claimed and made manifest, what the human being may know and be in reception to will be the Divine in all forms that it takes.

"Well, my career doesn't seem very divine, but I want a good career." Again, the small self says what she thinks she should have to confirm an idea of who and what she is. A career is not a bad thing, but it is not a requirement for growth or realization. You can have it or not. If it supports your realization or your evolution as a being, you can count on it coming in a way that you can learn through. But remember, friends, that how you learn and what you learn through is not always what the small self would decide she wants. You want the fine career, but then you get to learn why a career isn't so meaningful, once it has been claimed.

There is nothing you can encounter on the manifest plane that is not here to teach you, and as the will aligns with you to the True Self as its expression, your encounters with the manifest world will become rich in the awareness of the miracle of synchronicity. Now we will explain this. When the Divine will is operating in alignment with the small self, and then assumes the small self's will, you move into an idea of perfect order. "I am always where I need to be to learn what I came to learn."

This is done one step at a time, and not with a daily planner that reads for months at a time, or perhaps several years. You may only know the perfect order in the day you stand in. Everything beyond that is the small self's idea of projection. The claim we have given you—"I know who I am, I know what I am, I know how I serve"—will call you into present time when you seek to move beyond it to project in anxiety or desire, or in fear.

Now he asks a question. We must take it. "But are you saying we don't get to want anything? That sounds abysmal." You can want whatever you like. The alignment in will directs you and claims the True Self as wanting or requiring. You are actually getting support in realizing want through the braiding of the will, if what is desired is for the good or evolution of the being in desire.

Now there have been teachings that desire is wrong. We are not saying it's wrong, but it is misunderstood. You can desire a good meal or a good friend. These are things you may have and partake in. You are in a human experience where you need food and friendship. The idea of desire as claiming you and corrupting you is a rather different idea. "I must be the only one to climb to the top of the mountain. I must be the only one who gets what she wants."

Imagine that you are at a picnic under a great big tree. Everybody is invited to join the meal. There are no chairs or tables. There is a cloth upon the grass, and this cloth extends for a million miles. All are welcome to partake of the feast under the tree. It has been gifted to you to experience, but this is a shared communal experience. You are not hiding your picnic basket so that nobody else will steal your apples. You are not telling anybody that they are not allowed upon the blanket to share this feast. The manifest world has been gifting you each in your experience throughout lifetimes. It does not stop as you align in identity and in will with the True Self.

Now there are some desires, we would suggest, that move beyond the small self's needs to collective intentions. And these would be desires for fear, or to rule others, or condemn others, and you become complicit to the collective claim in fear as you align to it. The True Self will never align to any directive that would seek to condemn or control another. So you have an answer always when you ask, "How do I know if this is the True Self?" The True Self will never instruct you in fear, she will never damn a friend, she will never damn anyone. As you realize who and what you are, even those impulses, which are part of the collective wrath that you all agree to on a daily basis, are diminished and then absolved.

The netting that you have been caught in through collective agreement begins to break apart in the claim "I am free."

We will take a pause in a moment for Paul. Yes, this is in the text, and we would like to say to the reader, the welcoming we give you on this path, one flagstone, one step at a time, is that we are waiting for you every step of the way. You are not alone on this journey. How could you be? We are here. We are here. We are here.

Thank you, and stop now, please. Period. Period. Period.
(Pause)

We want to say a few things about their lives before this evening is over. They have been waiting for answers about what they do next. They were just given a teaching on what they can expect next through a braiding of the will and the assumption of the will by the True Self. In some ways what this does is release you from the responsibility of having to decide things right now. If you were to decide right now, in most cases, you would be deciding from the fear-based self seeking to control or claim a life in the way she has known. The gift of this teaching, as you accept it, is obedience in liberation.

"Isn't that a contradiction," he says, "obedience in liberation?"

In fact, they are the same thing. To be truly liberated is to be in obedience or agreement or coherence with the True

Self, who is your most trustworthy companion. If you would think that the Divine Self does not want you to enjoy yourself, you would be listening to a small self saying to the Divine Self, "You cannot be trusted. I will never have fun again."

The claim you make of freedom in alignment to the True Self gives you gifts. The first gift you receive is the awareness of who you are. And confounding the reality you have known, you continue to grow in unexpected ways. Underline *unexpected*. The growth of the True Self through you does not follow a course of action that could be prescribed by the small self in agreement to structure. How each of you evolves and claims anew and decides, we would suggest, will be claimed for you by the True Self, and your coherence to this is what brings your life forward. The issuance here—"I am free, I am free, I am free"—is a claim of liberation and obedience to the divinity that is inherent here.

Now he doesn't like the word *obedience*. "That sounds like a dog being trained. I don't want to be obedient. I want to have a nice life, enjoy myself in the remaining years I have. You know my list of desires. Let's meet them my way."

If you understood that true obedience is liberation, you are being obedient in your nonconformity. Do you understand that? You are being obedient to truth, and not to lies. You are being obedient to love, and not to fear. What great gifts these are.

If you want to have a reckoning in fear and continue to play that game out, you can, if you wish. You will learn that way and we will support you in that learning, if that is the best way to get you going. Learn in fear, by all means. But you don't have to. In obedience to love, you learn the lessons of love. In obedience to truth, you claim a world in truth. And joy, we would suggest, is as available to learn through as any other ideal or way of being.

We say thank you, tonight, for your attendance to our words thus far. The book that you are reading is a lengthy book, in some ways, because the lessons live long beyond the final page. The lessons of this book will be with you throughout your lifetimes, and the inherited wisdom you are attending to by your agreement supports you in your own knowing of what you are, who you are, and how you become what you are without fear.

So we say these words on this lovely day. We say yes, as you say yes, and now we say, good night. Period. Period. Period. Thank you, yes, in the book. Stop now, please.

Chapter Five

THE RAMIFICATIONS OF CHOICE

Day Seven

The choices you make that are claimed for you now will be operating in a different way than they have heretofore. You have an obligation now to the True Self. You made a choice, you claim in agreement, you are in coherence to the truth of the being of yourself. In this alignment so many things are possible that you cannot experience otherwise, and we must say to you, don't diminish your experiences now—because they will seek to escalate, they will seek to find themselves operating in higher ways. The temptation for some of you would be to hold up an umbrella to block you from the new sun that is shining upon you. You are used to the old dim light.

Now the consequences of choice, as we have taught you so

far, are infinite. The man winks at the woman. The woman winks back. Four hundred years later their progeny populate the world. The choice of the simple wink changed the planet, and the ramifications of the people on the planet, simply by nature of being, inform the field that the planet itself holds. So don't underestimate the choice you made here. It was far more than a wink, and your progeny, in some ways, will be everyone you encounter in the higher octave that you may now witness them in.

The choice to see another as the True Self comes with consequence, as well. Your desire to be right, to be told who you are by another, to be reaffirmed in any way, is diminished radically the moment you decide that the one before you—whoever he is to you, stranger, friend, or foe—is indeed the Divine Self, because they are, and that will never change. Your alignment to them in the higher way is what transmits the echo—"I am free, I am free, I am free"—in their field as well, because it is true at the level of the Divine Self, whatever that person is expressing as that you may not like or seek approval of. The True Self, you see, begins to encounter the True Self in others in this new field of liberation.

The idealization of who others should be to you must be understood now. Everyone you meet is there for you to meet, and whatever your encounter is will be informed by who you think they are. To move from thinking to knowing is much of the passage of this text, because in your knowing you are undefined by the qualities that would keep you in separation. You are unbound by the tethers that have been significant in limiting your expression.

So as you realize yourself, and you realize the one before you, you claim them outside of the known, which must include the quality of the relationships you have had thus far, which are once again informed by history. Let's look at history for a moment. Your idea of what happened is all that history is, at least in your own experience of it. "He was nice to me yesterday, I expect he will be nice to me today" would be a simple example about how you predicate behavior from someone else, based upon the moment you stand in, by what you call to you from the past through ideas.

History is an idea. We are not saying that things don't happen. We are not saying the earth is flat or round, although at different times people believed both those things and assumed that they were in truth. You believe you are on a plane now that is a planet bound by energy, but in fact where you are is in vibration, and as you realize that, the realization of what the world is in vibratory fields, or in octaves, begins to be understood by you outside of the claims of history. You know where you stand because you know the place on the map that was named by someone who decided the name long before you were born. You give their inheritance credence when you walk upon the road that they have named. When you decide that the only name of any town is the place you are, that the only bridge that you cross is between two ideas of landscape, you move beyond claims of history to realization and to knowing.

Well, this confounds Paul. "If I am on Main Street, I am on Main Street. If the bridge crosses to the next town, I am now in the next town."

You are only on Main Street because you are agreeing to that history. If somebody hid the sign, you would be on a street with no name. The bridge was built to allow passage between two landmasses. They are now known as towns. These towns were named by people through heredity, through the culture or time the town was initiated. You carry that history with you when you see the town by going into accord to it. This is a very simple teaching. There is nothing wrong with the name of the town, but it is history that you are confirming by agreeing to it.

In your relations, certainly things happen. People weep in a fight. "He is the man who made me weep, she is the one who made me angry" are ideas you have about perhaps who you are in coordination with the behavior of another. When you look at history in a larger way, in landscape or field, you begin to understand that if you were not naming history, your experience of wherever you are might be very different, and your interactions with anyone would be very different as well.

Now we are not saying things don't happen. Perhaps the man made you weep, perhaps the woman made you angry. That is not the issue here. The issue here is your definition of them through past acts or behavior that are primarily informed by your own ideas, or prescriptions, or intent to interpret behavior or what you would call history as what you want it to be. In fact, everything you see in every interaction can be interpreted in many ways. The man who made the woman weep meant to make her happy. The man that got angry meant to feel like a fool, and now look what he has done. The intent may not be what you think, but you experience the ramifications of the actions through your ideas of what is happening, or what happened historically between the two of you.

When you realize the Divine Self and you bring it to any interaction, it's not that you eradicate history, but you stop deciding based upon it in the awareness that the True Self knows and the small self's interpretation of any incident is informed by the history one holds. "He looked at me that way. My father looked at me that way once. I won't be seen as my father saw me." And you claim the history of prior relations in the present-day encounter, perhaps to the detriment of the relationship.

When the True Self encounters you, he actually encounters you beyond the boy who was scolded by his father to see the Divine being who was present then, at that time in history, and is present now, and will always be present. We don't negate the boy who was frightened by his father's anger. We realize the divine presence of the one we see before us, and in that claim—"you are free, you are free, you are free"— realize them, which means know them beyond the history that they are operating with or you are attempting to inform them with as a small self.

Now the Divine Self expressing as you does not operate through history. But, like anything else, the True Self may know the consequence of past behavior and, consequently, direct you to new opportunities. This will only happen if you are not deciding in history what you should do, or they should do, or how you should be with one another. Remember this, friends. Your interpretation of any event has been informed by you through the mirror that you have held, seeking to reflect what you want to see, or given the interpretation you assume it should have. So whatever the mirror says, whatever is reflected back to you, is actually claimed in some ways through a faulty lens born in history. "I was ridiculed as

I was a child. Now that I am an adult, I expect to see ridicule." There is no ridicule, except the one the man expects to see, and he will encounter it if he intends to.

We have given you this teaching prior—it is the teaching of the frame. The individual holds a frame of an idea of who he or she is, and then seeks to fill it in their experience. This is how the small self manifests, but it is also how the True Self operates. When the lens that is being presented, or the mirror that is being held high for reflection, is not tainted by history, you will know what is so. You will not seek to confirm what you would have confirmed to have your ideas about the world proved right. Your ideas about the world are just what they are—ideas. While there is nothing wrong with ideas, you do understand the difference of realization and knowing, and holding an idea to what something can be, or perhaps should be, or even better yet, what was.

You have collective ideas about the history of your world, which every hundred years or so is informed by new data, and you are expected to appropriate the data and re-conceive the world you live in. Every thousand years or so, all of your ideas are banished about where you are or what the world looks like. And if you can assume that will continue to happen, you will be very right.

It was not terribly long ago that the bulk of you thought the world was flat, patted yourselves on the backs for being right, and assumed that God was an old man in a cloud looking down on you, snickering at your bad behavior, and seeking to punish you for it. You have enlightened yourselves some, but not so much that you can't be surprised at what will be revealed to you when you understand that the claims that you have made have actually opened you up to possibilities in your experience that will bypass the laws that you have believed would always be there. The belief in time and how time operates, the belief in a physical world as not malleable to thought, the ideas you hold about gender identification—thoughts are things, whatever you may call them—will be transforming through your realization of liberation.

Now there is nothing wrong with time. It's a collective agreement that you operate with that serves you well as you need it. But imagine, for a moment, if there was no time. What would your experience be right now? There is no time. There has never been a clock invented. The shadows on the wall from the sun are just pretty pictures. They are not telling me what time in the afternoon it is. I am liberated from a structure that I have agreed to.

If you allow yourself to experience this, even for a moment, you will actually have an experience of timelessness. And the Divine Self we speak to, who is here, who is here, who is here, as we have said, exists beyond time but may operate in time as and through you. Once you understand that every structure that was created, even in your sciences, that you have confirmed may be transformed or re-understood in a new way, you will become available to what is always true.

The science of your year is utilized in the year you live in. Three hundred years ago, you had no electricity. The idea of it was preposterous. If you understand that you are still operating in a dark room, and you understand the lightbulb, but not the source of the light, you will also understand that the precipice you all stand on is magnificent change. Underline the word *magnificent*. But total change, we would have to say, comes at cost.

Those who believed the world was flat saw themselves as fools when the new information was revealed to them, and those who had a real investment in the world being flat sought to imprison those who said it was not. The same thing happens now in some ways. The investment in history, what you were taught to believe as true and are asked to confirm unknowingly by your agreement to it, is what is going to be directed now in a very different way than you have done thus far.

We are going to ask you, at your convenience, to make a list of things you were taught to believe about the world you live in. Whatever it may be, it is your list for your own benefit. And if you ask why you confirm these things, you will most likely find that you will be saying in response to them,

"I believed this because I was told it was true. It was confirmed by science or by law. I wanted to believe this was true, so I confirmed it. I agreed to what I was taught because who am I to disagree?"

We are not asking you to rethink science. We are asking you to put everything on the table—underline *everything*—that has been decided for you that you have not asked questions of, and then say, "Why do I agree to this?" Remember that agreement and coherence or vibratory accord are the same things. When you move out of accord with what you have been taught, then you can claim what is not known yet, or what has not taken form.

When you understand that the collective has agreed to war, and you believe that war will always be there because it's always been there, you understand an example of accord and history. Who says there was always war? And the idealization that there always has been continues war when there is no need for it. To move to an idea that there can be a world, or is a world, that exists beyond that level of agreement makes it so. War will not be claimed by one who is not in accord to war, who is not in agreement to it in vibration, who is not aligning to the history that says it should be there.

When the Divine Self claims someone else in freedom, you are not transforming the person's identity, you are claiming them outside of the behavior or wrong identification that they have operated with. When you realize the world in a higher way, the same thing occurs. A world without war is a world that is not confirming historical data that was born in fear that has claimed itself in the manifest plane and is perpetuated by all of you simply by your agreement to it.

"Well, I didn't make the war," you may say. But you are confirming it even in that statement, and to confirm war is to perpetuate it. The first step to move beyond this is to lift beyond the claims of history to the potential that there is peace, there is peace, there is peace, and in that agreement to be in peace you don't claim war because war does not exist in peace.

Now the ramifications of choice, which is in fact the title of this chapter, will be understood by you through your experiences. So our offering to you, and our plea to you, in some ways, is not to limit your experience by denying the potential that the changes that can come to you are quite radical. Remember the example that we gave you of the man holding the umbrella to block the brightness of the sun. He is used to shadow. He would prefer the shadow of the known to the brightness that is being revealed to him. The sun is still shining, with or without the umbrella.

If you decide today that you can access new levels of expression, new levels of experience, you can rely upon the new to support the claims you make and understand history as what it is—just an idea. Read your history books for an hour and you will see that they are slanted to the culture that dominates, and the history book seeks to affirm their view of what happened, where and when. If you look at a church and its investment in its politics, its desire to survive has created dogma that was never implicit in the original text. You are being used by confirming them to claim an idea that was just an opinion a long time ago.

The name of the town you stand in may have been the name of a man who lived here once. It may have been the name of a thing, or a rock, or an ash that fell from a fire. When you look at a town called Ember, you assume you know what it means, but the town of Ember, we would suggest, is simply an idea that you confirm when you look at the sign that tells you where you are.

Look at your lives, then, where you do the very same thing. "I am at this stage of my life. That is what this means. One day I will be at that stage. We know what happens at that stage. I understand that stage because I have been told what to believe." Again, the claim "I am free, I am free, I am free" supports you in this realization that you are not bound by history, but please ask yourself where you seek to confirm it out of the convenience of relying upon the old.

Once again, we say these words: "Behold. I make all things new." That is the True Self in its vision, in its expectation, so as you align to it, you may begin to receive its fruits. We will take a pause for Paul in a moment. We will continue this chapter at another time. Thank you for your presence. Period. Period. Period.

Day Eight

Now each of you comes with a decision you have made about what a lifetime is. In some ways these decisions are made prior to incarnation and then reinforced through the encounters you have in the lives you have chosen to live. Every encounter is an opportunity to learn through, and every choice you make will direct you toward the next one. In a life, there are many opportunities to claim victory over fear, and the teaching you will receive this weekend, in many ways, will be about the encounter with fear that must be claimed in order to move beyond it.

Many of you decide that what your lives should be is effortless, easy, without pain. And while we commend you for these things, you must also understand that being in a life is a great opportunity for the array of experience that may be met by you in each encounter. And the encounter with fear, which you have had with you since birth, must now be seen as something that can be moved beyond. But this will not happen if you don't agree to it.

The claims that you make in fear—"I will be known in a certain way, I will have my way at the cost of this or that"—are claims you make in your world. And the implications of each claim on those you meet reinforces the fear that has always been behind them. A decision made in fear will call more fear to it by energetic action and by agreement in vibration. When you yell at someone in your anger, which is an expression of fear, you claim the next response in vibrational accord. And the treason you convey against the Divine Self is the abnegation of its authority to claim a situation as it would, which is free from fear.

Please understand, friends, there is an aspect of you here who has always been, who will always be, who is unafraid and doesn't react or condemn or claim a life in fear. The small self does this in agreement to what she has known, who she has thought she was, or what he thinks the world should be. The Divine Truth of your being, who is unafraid, is who seeks to reclaim you, and as he does, as she does, you amass a frequency, a level of accord that will actually preclude you from taking actions in fear. As you announce this—"I am free, I am free, I am free," which is the freedom of the known and all that the fear has claimed—you announce yourself in a new world, a world that doesn't agree to fear because the vibration you hold will not align to it.

Each of you comes with an idea of what your life should be. In most cases, the idea that you have has nothing to do with the choice that was made prior to incarnation. Your idealization of the world in form, what you should want or aspire to, is what claims you instead. When you realize the True Self and its mission to be realized as and through you, you forget what you wanted as a small self. You deny the purview of the small self to claim in fear as the Source of her protection or agreement to a world that would have her be as it should.

The True Self, you see, doesn't care, and is unafraid, and in her love she will support you, the self you think you are, in a level of acclimation to a way of being that will actually support you in reinforcing her and her purview over everything you see. If you understand what this means, it's very significant. The realization of the True Self in form and field as you claims a world into being by energetic accord. The vibration you hold in agreement to be supports everything it sees in a re-acclimation to its true nature. If you understand that God is all things—name it as you wish, we use the word *God* here for a reason—you can understand that the realization of God in all things simply claims what is, in the higher octave that God expresses through. Every rock, every low being, or what you would call low, is of God, and your realization of the rock and the low being claims God as what it has always been.

But the vibration you support it in operates in a higher octave than what you have thought. You are literally lifting your world in vibratory accord through your presence and through your action of witness upon the world you see. You each identify, not only through the known, the known world, perhaps, but your ideas of what it means. This is very significant. Your ideas about the world are what claims the world, not so much how you see it, but how the ideas you invest in play out before you. It is why one man's shack is another man's castle. The shack itself is just an emblem, just an idea, but what the idea brings to it, home, sanctuary, hovel, or mud, will vary greatly dependent upon who sees and what ideas he or she brings to it.

If the world is just an idea—and we have to tell you that it is, the world is just an idea—your reclamation of the True Self in your identification claims the world as it has always been, the Divine in expression. The idea that you claim your world in vibratory accord is very accurate, but many of the teachings you have received are limiting. "I will create a house for myself to live in." "I will create a partnership to be married in." While these things may be claimed and can be, they are being claimed in a field of agreement to limitation.

When you understand that God is the partnership, or God is the home you buy, an expression of God manifested in form, everything begins to transform because you are no longer bound by law that would seek to express in limited ways. The desire you have for realization is not an agreement by the small self. The small self, in fact, wants things as they have been—some modulation, perhaps, to get away from some discomfort you have and say you no longer want. But the idea of being expressed in a higher world, and supporting the world you see in its manifestation in the higher octave you express through, is an anathema to the small self who cannot agree to this because she cannot live in the new world.

"What does this mean?" Paul asks.

As we have taught prior, the Kingdom, the realization of the Divine in all things, is met by you in co-resonance. The Divine Self is who exists at this level, and the Divine as you, the manifestation of you in form and field in vibratory accord, is what supports the claim of agreement that allows your entry. The small self, who is invested in fear, cannot enter the Kingdom because she is not in alignment to it. The exercise we bring you in this teaching is a reconciliation with who and what you are as it exists outside of fear.

Paul is interrupting again. "But can we exist outside of fear? This is a proclamation I can't agree to. I am afraid of many things. I can't imagine myself without fear, fear of this or that, and I am not alone. We fear famine, we fear war. What becomes of us when we are old and alone or infirm? What do we do? And are you saying that these things can be rid of?"

Yes, we are. We are saying that. But we must say the list that you just gave was the small self's agenda for keeping herself away, himself away, from her divinity and his True Self. Everything you listed was a denial of the Divine or the presence of God that can be known in form and agreed to in a higher way. By your list, you are saying, "There will always be war, there will always be famine, we may grow old alone and become infirm" as if these things cannot be met by you as the True Self in a vastly different encounter than you have aligned to thus far.

Your self-recrimination, which is the small self recriminating itself, is to blame here. You don't understand, after all of these teachings, that the God within is more powerful than fear. And if God is more powerful than fear, why would you say that there are things that cannot be met by God and manifested anew? This is the most simple teaching you will ever get. If God is present in manifestation, God may be known as manifest. If God is conjecture, a theory, a nice idea perhaps, some dogma to chew on, you will never have an experience of divine presence in manifestation. You have decided that theory trumps form, or the expression of the Divine as can be known in form.

So back to that list. If you want to have these things, these little honor badges of your fears that you parade around the world in—believe us, they are seen by all—you will understand that the manifest self, the True Self as you, can encounter them and lift well above them. When you were afraid of the dark when you were a child, you thought you would never outgrow it. Finally one day you did, and it has long been forgotten. You have acclimated to a place where that fear no longer resides. You don't expect to reclaim it. You prefer a dark room for sleep than a bright one. You have moved beyond what you thought you were to claim who you truly are as one who is unafraid.

These other fears that you know yourselves through are really no different. The big challenge is that you are invited to have them through a collective agreement that they will always be there. And the reinforcing of the collective will, the small self saying, "Yes, look what will happen to us all, this terrible blight, this terrible thing, we will all be killed," whatever it may be, not only confirms fear, but it becomes the vibration you hold and are in manifestation with.

As we teach you to triumph over fear, to lift beyond the agreements fear has made, we are also going to invite you to say yes to what can be without, and your agreement to be without will become the basis for the next chapter of your life. "If I am no longer frightened of this, what am I? If I was no longer frightened to be this, who will I be? If I can, will I? If this can be claimed, may I? May I know? May I be? May I be in this encounter with the Divine that I know in my heart is present in all manifestation?"

The willingness is the willingness to step upon the grass when the sign says, "Don't tread here." The willingness is the willingness to say yes in the face of a world that would call you mad. But the agreement is such a simple one. "I am no longer willing to live in fear. I am no longer willing to abide in fear. I am no longer willing to claim myself as the one who is afraid." In this agreement, you pull the lever on the mechanism that is you to move toward great transformation.

Now we must address the idealization of fear, which operates with you, again, in collective accord. The belief that you each have that you are protected by your fear must be abandoned today. What does it mean to be protected by fear? "Well, if I speak to those people I may be harmed; if I go to that country, I may be harmed; if I listen to this teaching, I may be harmed; I will not go, I will not meet, I will not listen" and claim the small self in purview by that choice to be expressed in limited ways. The action of fear is to claim more fear, and this agreement to be free from fear will be met by resistance because there is an aspect of you that believes that the cloak of fear will protect her from the terrible things that would come if one is exposed to the light.

What do you hide? What do you covet? What do you claim in fear? What don't you want your friends to know about how you really think of them? The small self's agenda in fear is to protect all things and present the self that will get her what she wants. Do you all understand this? The small self's agenda is to protect herself and to get what she wants, because what she wants affirms her being. And if what she wants is to be told that she should be ashamed, or she should be lauded, or he should be seen as the best or the worst, the small self will seek to claim it from every encounter that he or she has.

When there is no fear to operate from, you move to authenticity. You are no longer playing the part that you think you have been assigned. You are no longer agreeing to the small self's desire to manipulate her world to reinforce the idea of who and what she is as was prescribed for her by her family, or time or date of birth, and the culture she grew up in. Once you become free of your relationship to fear as your savior, as your protector, you cannot be lied to because you will not be in resonance to lies yourself. You have become witnessed as what you are, the True Self in form and field who has come to claim a world.

Yes, this is in the text. We will continue this teaching in

different ways as we teach, and, as we deliver this teaching, we have an intention for all of you who hear these words. You will be known by us without fear, and because we agree to know you without fear, you can claim it in the field you hold. The octave that you express in when you are not operating in fear is not the octave that you have been living in. It is not the octave where you worry if the bills are paid or the husband is faithful or the children are excelling in school. It is not the octave where you rage against a structure that is not doing what you want. It is the level where all of these things will be seen and known in a higher way, and, as a result of that witness, your relations to them will be greatly transformed.

"How is this done?" he asks. "How will you know us without fear?"

By claim, and by claiming truth. The truth of who you are is unafraid. The frequency you hold is an expression of you. When the Divine Self is claimed in fullness, fear is not present, it has no place to live, and the memory of fear, which may be useful to you in your navigations of this plane, simply becomes what it was—a memory, an idea that you no longer embark upon. It is not a cinder that you blow into a fire. It is ash that you recall, and you nod, and you say, "Yes, that is what was, but now it is all new."

"Is this possible?" he asks. "Don't take us someplace where you can't deliver the goods."

You are the goods, my friends. You are the goods. You are being delivered.

And that is the end of this teaching. Period. Period. Period.

(Pause)

Each of you comes with the ability to transform your world through your encounter with it. Understand these words. You have the ability to transform your world through your encounter with it. Everything you see and encounter is there to be seen, and perhaps re-seen in the higher octave that the True Self abides in.

What does it mean to re-see? To re-conceive or re-perceive what you thought was to what is and can only be in the higher octave that you have aligned to. When you see something and you bring your ideas to it, you make it good or evil. You decide its merit, or worth, or lack thereof. You decide what things mean through your prescriptions and identifications. When you see something anew, you are being invited to release the history that you have endowed the ideas with. "This is good or evil, right or wrong." These are things that are known by you. Some may be true, perhaps, but many of them are prescribed for you.

When you have neutrality and you perceive something without the conditioning you have inherited, you have the opportunity to re-conceive. This isn't about re-deciding what you feel about what you see. It's about deciding that the narrative that you have attached to the thing, the object of your perception, has had to be revealed in another way.

The emotional attachments to what you see inform what you see, yes, but in fact they are secondary because your emotional responses are the benediction and the referred issue of how you have idealized something. "Look at that dead cat, what an ugly thing to see" or "what a sad thing to see" or "what a beautiful thing to see, that cat was suffering, we are pleased that she has departed." Your ideas of the dead cat are claiming you in emotion, either disgust or fear or celebration, whatever it may be. How you perceive the cat and are endowing what you see with ideas predicates the emotional response. "Look at that lovely wedding. They all look so happy. They will have a lovely life." "Look at that awful woman. She is marrying that man for his money. I hope it lasts a week. He will figure her out as I have." The wedding may be witnessed by two parties in two different ways and claimed in two different ways. Whatever you see, you are deciding the meaning of, and relying upon history informed data to tell you what it should mean.

When you look at an example of war or conflict, you are immediately siding with one group or the next, depending on where you stand. And who is good or evil or what the outcome should be is still being prescribed by you in relation to the ideas you hold. What if you could look at a war as an event in neutrality? What would become of the reason you see? How would you invest in the picture you see if the outcome wasn't required to be any certain thing? Now we are not lauding war. We are neutralizing it only for the purpose of this exercise. To see something and release your investment in outcome or ideology to simply see it as it is gives you the opportunity to re-perceive it. And by re-perception or re-seeing, we are actually telling you that you may reclaim it and your relationship to it in a way that will not only transform it, but its repercussions upon the world before you.

When you witness a man and you decide his merit based upon his clothing or his perceived occupation, you have decided for him, not only in relationship to you, but in relationship to the world that he exists in. You are actually claiming him in a landscape, and how you claim anyone has repercussions upon the landscape itself. When you see the man without the clothing or the occupation, when you don't decide his well-being from how the body looks, or his age, or the color of his hair, you have an opportunity to perceive the man in a new way. We are not denying the color of his hair, or the wrinkles on his skin, or the shape of the body. We are simply saying you are not investing meaning in those things and calling your heritage about what a body should be or what age looks like to the significance of that man. He simply is. Because he is, he may be known anew. You are not fixing him. You are conceiving him in truth. When you conceive another in truth in this way, you are realizing him beyond the small self's prescriptions of what should be, or how he must be to suit your need or investment about what kind of a man he should be. The true man, the true being that he is, is now being witnessed and known in a higher way through the claim of truth you give him.

Now when we give you the opportunity to be witnessed by us, when we say the words to all of you—"We know who you are in truth, what you are in truth, how you serve in truth"—we are doing just this. We are not standing there before you thinking about your lineage, or your religious up-bringing, or how you should do your hair, or how you should pray, or confirming what you think you should be. We are seeing you beyond those things, and through bearing wit-ness in this regard we support you in co-resonance with us in the higher octave that we express as. As you are as us in real-ization, what you are then able to do through your uninvest-ment or release of expectation about who others should be or what others should do, or an outcome you would have seen based upon your prescriptions of what the world should be, you are allowing the possibility that your presence and wit-ness will realize what is beyond the ideology or reasons or motives that you have attached to what you see before you.

You see that man. "He looks like that kind of man. I

assume he wants this or that from me." And you are prescribing who he is in the landscape that you share, and you have decided your relationship to him in a low vibration. To become neutral to the man cannot be done at the level of the small self, but it is done by the True Self, who is the only one that can claim "I know who you are in truth." This is not about getting people to behave. It is about realization and knowing.

Now the fabric of reality that you share is malleable to thought, and this is what you don't understand. How you perceive anything informs the object of your perception. How you perceive as the True Self informs the object at that level of agreement or co-resonance, and in fact lifts it to where you have aligned to as the perceiver. When a collective of people re-conceive someone or something without historical data or reprimand, enforcing the vision, the one that is seen by the collective itself is lifted in a way to be re-known.

"What does this do to the man?" Paul asks. "Isn't just seeing someone a nice thing?"

A re-conception of anything supports the possibility that it may be known in a very different way. Imagine you have a house with two bedrooms and an attic and a cellar. You place your furniture in the rooms where you think it should go, based upon where the walls were erected. You assume what's in the house are where things should be, based upon the model of the house and the placement of the walls. If you remodel the house, you re-conceive it. It may now have an additional story, or no basement. The attic may become a rumpus room, and you may have a window where there was once a wall.

When something is re-known, it must take a new form, and the new form the man takes, who is being witnessed by the collective, is who as the man is, can only be, at the higher octave. We will explain this for Paul. You exist in multiple dimensions or octaves, as we like to say. The manifest self is in a shared plane of experience with your fellows. You know each other by the agreement to the landscape you share—"where we go to school, where we go to work, what we see in the sky." These are shared agreements, and there is a shared narrative that reinforces the reason that all these things are. The collective expects what the collective has had.

As you lift to the higher octave, what you begin to see is that the transformation of a reality is predicated upon the individual and his perception. Only the one who sees the truth can speak the truth. Only the one who knows the Divine Self can witness the Divine Self in all she sees before her. And the re-acclimation of the landscape in participation with the individual is what we are teaching you now. If you can understand that when the collective begins to shift its agreement to past narrative, what things have meant or should mean, to see the truth, the recognizable truth, the man without the occupation and the clothing that would define him, the collective will realize the man in a higher way because they are not embellishing the old or deciding what the new should be.

When we witness you and we claim you are free, we are claiming what is always true—underline the word *always*—in the higher octave. Because we recognize you in the higher octave, without your ideas of who you are standing in the way, you are lifted by us in co-resonance and benefit. If you agree to this, it happens quite easily.

What is happening in the world now is that the idealizations of structures, things that you have counted upon to be there, are being dismantled. Your idealizations of a government, or a banking system, or what culture means in inherited ways are being re-seen and disassembled in many ways so that the new can be claimed. You cannot claim the new when your investment in the old is paramount. You will do everything that you can to defend the old structure, decide it should be there because it always was.

Let's go back to the man that the collective is seeing, naked and without employment. He can be anything. Do you understand this? He can become an astronaut. He can become anything because the potential is not realized because it has not been decided by you. If you have a man who operates in fear, and you witness him in truth, and you move beyond the fear, what you do is give him permission to realize truth at the cost of the old. It's not that you are denying the fear, it's that you are witnessing the man without it because you are witnessing him without the embellishment, or established ideology, or meaning that you would have endowed him with through the historical data that you use to perceive anything.

"Back to war," Paul asks. "You can't give us that example and not tell us how war transforms."

When you uninvest in the meaning of something, you can claim it in a higher way. To reinforce how terrible something is doesn't transform it, it confirms the terrible nature. To see something in a new way is to give it the potential to be transformed. The ideology that you hold that the men on the battlefield will meet each other in death denies the possibility that they may meet each other in embrace. Do you understand the difference? Your confirmation of what can be affirms a future where you get what you expect.

Can you imagine a battlefield with men fighting where music begins to play, and all the men begin to hear the music that could not possibly have been there, and respond to the music in a dance? Can you imagine what happens when the weapons fall to their side because they are no longer agreeing to what they were doing, but being confirmed by a different experience—in this case a strange music, another idea, if you will—that is now being imprinted in the collective field that they have shared. The Divine Self is the music, and the claim of it for them—"I know who you are in truth, what you are in truth, how you serve in truth"—renders them without the uniform and the expectation of battle. Do you understand this? They are all the men that wore the suit, that had the occupation, that you stripped down and saw as potentially transformed.

When you see a war, you are seeing an idea being engaged with in actual ways. It is only the idea that is forcing the men into the ballet of destruction. If the idea is changed, the music is changed, and the dance changes as well. When the world itself decides, decides, decides that war means nothing and grants nothing to the victor, the possibility of a world without war will exist. But because you bring your decision about what things should be to your witness of the narrative, you end up confirming the very things that you say you don't want to see.

Paul asks a question. We will have to answer this one. "Will we ever know a world without war?" When there is no one left to fight, you will. If you continue on the path that you are on, that will be how you know the end of war. If you wish to transform that option, you must understand the futility of it and that the Divine in the Divine that is you knows the Divine that is in all else. The God within you knows the God within all else. And the God within you, whatever you wish to call it, will not confirm war because it does not exist in the higher octave that it does.

The work we do with our students is to lift them beyond the agreements made through historical data to freedom, and in this place we are supporting you all in the reclamation of the landscape you exist in as the Kingdom. Underline the word *as*. The Kingdom is here, but is only witnessed by one who knows who she is, and in your witness of the landscape you share, you lift the world you see to its truth—the Divine in the Divine in manifestation in all you encounter.

If you wish, take a moment today and witness anything, a leaf on a tree, a man on the street, a child at play, an argument or a war, and release your investment in narrative, what you endow meaning with and claim in emotional response to. See it in neutrality, first and foremost, and then say these words: "I know who you are in truth, I know what you are in truth, I know how you serve in truth. I see you in truth and lift you by this agreement to your true nature."

See what you feel and experience, and understand, friends, that you are the emissary to support the world in its knowing of what it is through your witness. Period. Period. Period. Stop now, please.

(Pause)

When you decide that the life that you live has moved beyond the need for fear, you recognize the potential that can be claimed by you in all aspects of your life. So much of your life has been informed by fear that you take it as a companion. "Who would I be if I was not afraid? I take comfort in my fear. I know myself well as fearful, and consequently I will take it out to tea." Your fear as your companion.

Understand this, friends, the Divine as what you are is your true inheritance, and your obligation to it—and we use that word intentionally—is to give it permission to become as you. Underline the word *as*. *As* you are. And its realization, its purview as the what that you are, tells it very quickly that fear is no longer welcome, not a welcome companion, not a welcome guest in your life.

In order for this to be known as so, you must understand that you are not fear, and fear is not you. "I am fearful or full of fear" may be a descriptor that you would use to say what you are or how you are investing in an idea of yourself, but it is also not saying that you are fear. Fear is a distinct energy from the True Self, and, as we have said many times, at the level of the True Self, fear does not exist.

Now you don't excise fear as you would a splinter from the foot. You don't say no to fear as you would a wayward child—"Not today, fear, I am in no mood for you"—which simply implies that it is going to obey you for a short while.

The realization of the True Self, who does not align to fear, is in fact what claims you in liberation: "I am free," freedom from fear and all of its creations.

Now what a creation is, is a thing made, either in vibration, or then in form. You have things in vibration that may never manifest in the material realm in solidified ways. But much of what you understand yourself as—"I am the one who worries" or "gets confused"—are energetic assumptions that you prescribe a reality to as you experience yourself as confused or afraid. "I become the idea of what I am."

But other things become manifest or made in form—the roads you drive on, your schools. All those are, are energetic ideas that were claimed in form and have adherence in collective value. We all see the school, we all know where the road goes. Your ascription to what you are, your idealization to what you think you are, is also a creation, and the bodies you know yourselves through, while in form as you, are also malleable to thought and intention.

"Well, that does not make sense," he says.

In fact, it does. You all ascribe to a passage of time. You know how many months make a year. You know youngsters from the elderly. You participate in the manifestation or out-picturing of form through the collective realization of what life should be. If in fact form is malleable, it is malleable to consciousness, and the happy man may realize himself in a happy life and his form may well reflect it. The idealization of form as needing to resemble something or other must be understood by you as collective agreement as well. The species that you know yourselves as are integrating your potential into the material realm. Potential is first known in higher octave, and then made manifest in flesh and bone.

"How does the species transform?" he asks.

Your consequence, the being that you are, is the consequence of many things. You understand your genetics and the pollution in your environment as contributing to the idea of what you are. "I am the one who does not breathe well, the air in this town is poor." "I have my father's poor eyesight and my mother's mean temper." You understand heredity as the basis for many things, but you don't understand that the higher alignment, that is now at present realizing itself as and through you, will actually collude with the physical form you have taken to re-identify itself as the expression of the Divine that it can only be in truth.

When something is known in the higher octave, it must be in resonance at that level, and the species you are, as it begins its journey in consciousness—or ascension, if you wish—must hold a form that will support the identity that it has taken. Now this does not mean you walk around in an idealized fashion. It does mean that the facilities that you have to comprehend your landscape must be informed with the necessary equipment to interpret the higher vibration.

Imagine you move to a mountain town way up there at the top of the Alps. The population of this town does not get dizzy walking out of doors, they have acclimated to the vibration of the higher field that they are partaking in. The air is fine to them, but those of you who come from the deep valley below will be gasping for air because you are not acclimated to the finer realization that exists at that level of occupancy.

Now some of you decide that what being the higher self means, or should be, will look a certain way. You will respond to things happily all day long, you will be in a perfect body, never get a cold, never lose your temper, and you will be happy all day long because the universe is supporting you in getting everything you want when you want it. That is not what happens, dears, and we are sorry to disappoint you.

You become what you truly are, the individualized expression of consciousness in form, and the form itself must align to the requirements that it is inheriting in the higher octave. If you get a cold, you won't be complaining all day, but if you walk out in the rain without an umbrella, you are sure to get wet, just as the one beside you is. You have emotional lives and emotional responses. It's part of what makes you so wonderful. You are not denied your full expression; however, you are not responsible for the ramifications of others' actions as you are accountable to your own response to them.

What this means is that your emotional lives are not subject to the being a certain way, idea, that you may have presupposed so far, but instead you are having expression in the brilliance of experience. Everything on this plane is to be experienced and encountered and known, but you may experience this plane in a higher octave than you have imagined you could.

"So how do our faculties change?" he inquires.

In several ways. The sensitivity you hold that you have believed to be your purview becomes a tool to realize others, or to know the requirements of the development of others as well. You become sensitized beyond the small self's needs to the needs of the community or the world itself. In fact you become, not a lightning rod, but a tuning fork for the vibration of the Divine. And because your vibration is always in expression, it is aligning everything that it encounters to its requirements for its own evolution. You become, in some ways, the one who knows.

Now understand this, friends. To be in your knowing at this level does not require you to choose for other people. Everybody has free will, and to know what another requires does not mean you give it to them. To realize another as who he or she truly is transmits the vibration from the higher vibration to them in a way that they can claim and assume as themselves. And this is done, not through deciding for others what they should be, but claiming what they are.

The agreement you make to become realized or known as the True Self has vast requirements. We could fill three more books with the requirements of this level of alignment, but the easiest way to understand is that what you are, in recognition of your world, will make no claim upon another but one that is in love. You are the emissary of the vibration of love, and the claim you make for another will be in agreement to this.

As we taught you in *The Book of Truth*, the frequency of truth in its neutrality will re-create and pave the way for love. When you operate in love, you are beyond distortion, and the only distortion you really face is fear itself. Now the requirement of fear is stasis, or what it could have in its final victory, which would be annihilation of the divinity that it holds. The small self holds divinity, but fear would deny it. The recognition of the Divine Self claims itself in opposition, not by the truth, but from the lie that it encounters. Truth is never afraid. It simply is. But when you shine a light, or the light of truth, upon what has been buried in the darkness, you will find that what has been hiding would seek to run from the light.

The process you are engaging in now, in vibration and

agreement as this light is shown through you, is the release of those things that have been hidden and have a great investment in remaining in the dark. We will offer you this now to support you in the passage that you will all undergo. There is nothing that can be encountered in fear that cannot be reclaimed in truth. There is nothing that can be seen in fear that cannot be re-known in truth. There is nothing that could be said or claimed in fear that cannot be reclaimed in truth. And the claim you make here—"I am free, I am free, I am free"—is the announcement of this light that will overshadow and repeal and dismantle those very things that would seek to claim you in the darkness.

The Divine as what you are cannot be concealed and will not be hidden, once it is announced as who and what you are. The triumph of the new comes at the cost of the old, and the challenges you will face through your participation in this learning are the things you would seek to hide being re-seen, re-known, and rearticulated in a higher way. "Behold, I make all things new."

Now we will say these words on your behalf, and we will say them with love:

"On this day we choose to witness all who hear these words as on a journey of reclamation. As the True Self ascends and reclaims itself in form and field, the release of the old is accompanied by love, and agreement to be in love. And the shadows of the past will be removed by the light of truth that would seek to realize itself through all mankind. We know who you are in truth. We know what you are in truth. We know how you serve in truth. You are free. You are free. You are free."

To be truly free is to be free of fear, and all of its creations, and all the lies that you have told yourself, or been told, that would collude with fear to keep you in fear or from the truth of your being. This is the day and the moment in this text where we announce you as what you have always been in the higher octave as free of fear, free of the web that fear has made about this plane, and free of the claims of it, of you, and of your world.

The announcement we make is an announcement of love, and the activation at this level of attunement will be rapid to those of you who accept it in potential. And these are the words we will speak, and we will invite you to speak them as well after we speak them:

"On this day I choose to realize myself outside of the bindings of fear, and by this claim, I call forth all support that is respecting my ability to ascend to this choice of manifestation. On this day I say yes to all that will support me in the realization of the True Self that exists without fear. I know who I am. I know what I am. I know how I serve. And I am free."

Be as you are, and know that this is so. Be received by us as we ascend with you to the level of vibration where the idea of fear itself no longer holds you or can claim you, and its inheritance is released from your field in perfect ways.

We say yes to each of you, and we say thank you each for your agreement to be free, free, free, free, free. Period. Period. Period.

Day Nine

We are here for you each on this journey you have chosen to take to the True Self as your full expression. Underline the word *full*. What does it mean to be in full expression as the True Self?

The Infinite Soul that you have has taken different forms in many incarnations. You have utilized these lifetimes as opportunities to learn and to create and to know yourself in a myriad of ways. The lifetime you are in now presents itself to you as an opportunity to be realized in fullness. Now by *fullness* we mean full expression—not the absolute, but the full expression of the Divine as you. The idea of an absolute expression reunites you in absolution with your Source. In fact, what happens then is that the being that you are is merged in entirety with the Source of its being, and while consciousness is present, it is no longer individuated. In some ways, you become the echo of God, with God, through all manifestation. The idea of singularity, which you are so attached to, does not exist, finally, at this level of expression.

But to be fully realized as who and what you are claims you still with identity and with the potential to grow and learn. This is not the last lifetime for most of you, and the True Self that you are will manifest to the degree of fullness that the vehicle you hold can attend to. If you manifest beyond what you can claim, you will become confused. The identity you hold will become scattered in pieces. You will differentiate the high and the low, yes, but the increments of expression that we have been offering you are to build your amplitude to the highest you can hold, so that you hold the identity you have in the highest way it can be attended to while in form and navigating a shared plane of expression.

We don't deny your individuation. We celebrate it, in fact. We celebrate the achievements of this plane, all that has been made in love, all that has been known in truth, and we understand the craziness that you attend to in trying to sort out who and what you are in a dense field that seeks to claim you and decide for you who and what you should be.

The reason we come and have come to this teaching in agreement with you is that humanity must now take a step in its inheritance and reclamation of identity. The Divine as what, the manifest self, is what is being known by you now. This is the next stage of creation on this plane of experience.

Now holiness, the Divine in all things, can be understood theoretically. "If there is a God, God is the star above me and the earth below. I understand the conception. But I don't agree to the experience of the cloud or the earth or the sea as of God, although I assume they must be." The re-creation of the physical self in manifestation to be holding the level of vibration commensurate to the higher octave we sing to you from is what aligns you to align this plane of expression to a higher nature. Underline the word *realization*. To *realize* is to know, and to know what you are is to be in *realization* of it. And, until you are in realization of yourself, the Divine as what you are, you will not realize the sea, or the star, or the blade of grass, or the air you are breathing as God itself. If all things are of God, all things may be known in this way, and they will be known, we say, by the one who has realized the truth of their being.

Full expression, identity as one with the True Self, not to

kill the small self, but to enfold it, absorb it, be as it, as you, in the highest realm you can align as—there is great significance to this teaching at this time, on this stage of this plane's evolution. Mankind, in its desire to claim separation, has created the means to absolve himself of any accountability for further growth, and we only say this at the level of the earth plane's expression. If you pollute your seas, if you kill your fellows, there is nothing more to do. If you stand in a landscape that cannot support life, the school that you have chosen to be in must shutter doors. Now the reason we say these things is not that it will happen, it's that the opportunity is being created at this time for true manifestation to claim you and all you see in the higher octave, because it is required now for humanity to claim independence from the creations of fear that see you as separate from the Source of your being.

The Divine as what, the claim of the Divine in form—"I know what I am"—makes manifest a level of vibration in the field, in the soul, in the body itself, that you may align to a new level of expression, and then meet your world in that congruence. The identity you have known yourself through, while intact, is no longer embedded with the fear that has sought to keep you in denial of your true heritage. The times you stand in are ripe for change, and glorious change, we would say, if you can feel the winds that are coming. They may tear from the trees, from the branches, those things that have stopped them from seeing full expression. The True Self, you see, is bold, is glorious, and his branches reach to the sun, and without impediment he may be known as one in his awareness of who and what he is in a great legacy. What is a legacy, but a lineage, and humanity itself is sovereign and always has been in its choice to be. The idealization of free will, in some cases, has been confounding for you. You assume your will is singular when humanity itself holds a collective will, and the collective will now, in a higher way, is claiming, yes, its true nature, its divine heritage. And the manifestations of fear that have obscured this are being torn from the branches of the trees that would block the sun.

A great wind, we say, has come to this plane. You may hide from the wind, you may be carried by the wind, you may glory as the wind strips your clothes from you and leaves you exposed in your own relishing of truth. You can stand by and hold the nearest flagpole and assume that your government will protect you from change. Everything will change because everything does. Your idea of safety has always been the known, but we promise you the new, if claimed in true accord, will be far better than what you have agreed to thus far.

The claim of freedom, "I am free," the utterance of these words themselves, is a challenge for many of you. You look at your lives, your creations, the pains that don't seem to go away, the fears that have been there since childhood, and you say, "No, I am not, I will not be lied to, I am not free." And in that claim, what you do is you close the shutters, sit in your room, and you wait for the wind itself to take your house, and perhaps you in it, to the next stage of change while you hide from the outcome. Perhaps the answer is to open the shutters, stand by the window, and say, "Yes, I see the change in my world, and I know in my heart that the result of change, and the result of truth claiming all things, will be a higher landscape, even if I have to trod over the ruins of what was claimed in fear for some time to come."

Why do you think it is better to protect the old and the known when you agree that the old and the known are horrible? Why do you decide to claim the known when you say you don't want it? There is only one reason—complacency, which is another mask of fear. "I really don't have to do this work. The world is going to change anyway." And, in fact, it will. And doing the work, we suggest, is simply being willing to be in the response to the requirements of truth as you are met by them. We have never asked you to renounce anything. We would never do that. We understand your need for the creations you have made. But until you individually—and, yes, collectively—decide to transform, which requires the release or renunciation of what has been held in fear, you will see yourself in an ongoing path claiming yourselves as separate from your fellows and the Source of all things.

The True Self, who is unafraid, becomes the aspect of you through realization that encounters the new world and claims the new in agreement to it. Remember, friends: Because the True Self does not operate in fear, it will not claim what is fearful. Why would it? Why would you claim the Divine and then be suffering from the claim you have made? Your willingness to attend to what is brought to you, what your soul itself is claiming for you to learn through, will be what you get as a transition toward the new.

Now an individual may see herself as needing certain things to maintain an identity or a way of being in the world. She will assume that what she has thought she needed will be what is required for a transition. In fact, when you have made the claim "I know who I am in truth, I know what I am in truth, I know how I serve in truth, I am free, I am free, I am free," you have broken all the rules anyway in terms of the small self's expectations. And your reliance upon the old to be your teacher is being removed by you—underline the word *by*—because it is no longer a requirement for your transitioning forward.

What instead comes is what the soul requires to learn through and what the True Self needs to realize itself as you through. Do you understand this? While the soul progresses through its lessons, the True Self seeks realization, and the illumination of the soul, the embodying as the soul and manifest in form is the Christed Self in alignment to a physically realized world. What this means is that the Divine Self in realization exists in a different world, a different environment of vibration than she could claim as a small self.

Now we will explain something for Paul. The soul itself progresses, as we stated. The Christed Self, Eternal Self, True Self, what have you, realizes itself through the expression that the soul has taken, and that is the life lived. When we say that the life itself calls to it what it requires, we are saying that, as you have chosen to align and embody, what is called to you are the requirements for that realization, which is why you don't attack things. You field them. It is why you receive change and you don't take a hammer to dismantle the old as much as let the wind come and let change be done.

The True Self is not passive. Far from it. But he does not rely upon the old tools to manifest change. He understands who he is, and his claim of freedom, "I am free," is a clarion call for transformation in his being and his expression, and consequently the environment he finds himself in.

Each of you who comes to us has decided at a certain level to be in this encounter with destiny. And your true destiny, we suggest, is realization in fullness, at this stage at least of your evolution. Absolution—to be as of the absolute without form or a name—is a wondrous thing, and some of us here know ourselves in this alignment as we can claim it in response to the wholeness, the totality of being. But the dimensions we exist in do not operate as yours do, so for us to explain how we navigate the fields or the octaves that are present here would be beyond your agreement at this stage. Eventually, we suggest, we will be able to claim these things through Paul in language we may attend to. But, for the time being, please accept the fact that what we speak is true, and your realization as what you are in manifestation is what claims the world anew.

The claim of service—"I know how I serve"—in some ways, yes, is the reason for this text, because all are called forward at this level of expression in service simply by nature of being. But in manifestation this becomes so, not through the small self's assertion that she will grow spiritually through service. Perhaps she may, but her motives may not be true. You may grow in spirit and in understanding through any encounter—through love, or loss of love, through birth and death. Your teachers are all around you. They need not resemble a manifestation that perceives itself as spiritual, because there is nothing on this plane that can be experienced that is not spiritual.

Your identity as a true being is what knows this to be so. The small self still looks for the attaché case with the instructions of how to be a spiritual being in the workplace with the benefits attached to it. The Divine as what you are exists beyond these things, but may know herself through all things, and until you understand that your being itself, the very being that you are, is what claims the world anew, you will be hunting for the instruction manual until you are in your next lifetime. Period. Period. Period.

Now this is not the end of this teaching, but this will be the end of this section. We are saying this for Paul, who is asking, "Does this stay in the text?" Of course it does, and more will come soon, and we thank you each for your attendance to these words. We will return shortly and resume. Period. Period. Period. Stop now, please.

(Pause)

Trust yourselves, please, to be in this encounter with the unknown. The release of fear that we speak to will have significant impact on the being that you are, and, consequently, the life that you live. When you release something that you have known yourself as, you are actually releasing what you think is you that has never been you. And if you can imagine an aspect of you that would fight to be known, and fight to be claimed, this is what you are asking to release.

Paul is interrupting already. "But do we love this aspect of ourselves? Is this how we release?"

You can love it if you like, you can accept it if you want, but you must also understand that the agreement that this was you, which was not an agreement made in truth, will be what allows you to decide to let it go. This is not you. You are not fear, and if you want to claim your fear—"Oh, thank you, fear, for protecting me from the terrible world outside"—you will have a lot more fear to come. To release fear is to say, "I am not fear, I am far greater than fear." If you think the fear is an aspect of you and not something outside, you will have a very hard time cleaning the dust off the windowpane. The dust is not the windowpane, but it might like you to think that it is so you don't go about washing it away.

When we ask you this—"Are you your fear?"—what is the answer you get? If we ask you a second question—"Why do you want fear?"—what is the answer you get? When we ask you the third question—"Are you willing to let this go?"—what is the answer you get? If the answer is "Yes, I am willing to let this go," we will do the work with you, and we will do it in a way that will reclaim you outside of fear.

Paul is asking, "My body is getting cold. I feel cold energy. Is this safe? What am I experiencing?"

You are feeling fear, and it is not you, and if you want to know yourself in fear, this is what it is like. You must have the experience of fear to know that it is not true. Paul, we say this to you. Allow the energy you feel to be where it is, so you may understand that this is what releases. It is not pretty, it is not comfortable, it is not what you want, you are not going to love it away. You can claim freedom from its purview, and it will know itself as having permission to release.

The claim of fear—"You will be as I am"—will not be known in the face of God. The claim—"You will be what I am"—will not be met in the higher octave of truth. The claim—"You will be what I am"—will not be agreed to by the True Self, who knows who he is, who knows who she is, and will now become the manifest self.

We will say these words for all of you who hear these words, and, as we speak them, we anoint you each in the higher octave where fear cannot claim you:

"On this day, we know each one in this encounter as free of fear. On this day we claim each one who hears these words as in liberation from the manifestation of fear that has assumed you and lied to you and convinced you you have no right to be what you are. On this day, we say yes to the realization of the Divine Self in fruition, in manifestation, in the claim of freedom that is here to be sung. I am free. I am free. I am free."

Let the release around your body come. Let the release from the field come. Let the claim of truth be made for you each. You are free. You are free. You are free. And as we sing these words to you, we align you to the what that you are, who exists out of fear, who has never known fear, and who will serve you in all ways. The Divine as what, the Kingdom, and the claim of the Kingdom has been made so.

Paul is asking, "What has happened here?"

What we said to you is you cannot be this and know that, and the energy around you and the students of this work is ashift, at times, in the recognition of this truth. In this moment, in this eternal moment, whenever you hear these words, or read them on the page, it is true. The Divine what, the true what, the claimed True Self in liberation, is realizing itself at the cost of fear. There is nothing they need to do. They don't need to claim it. They agreed to it. They said the words to themselves, if they wished. The choice was made, and may be made again as required.

For you, Paul, we have to tell you that what is clearing from your field is what you have been waiting for—the gift of freedom from the small self's claim of abnegation, of betrayal, of all the things he has thought could be in fear, the release of the names he has used to define himself in separation from love. The Divine as what does not hold these things.

The small self, you see, has done his very best in the ways that he could to know himself as free, but it's as if the small self were in the briar patch, and every attempt toward liberation, every attempt of escape, resulted in more wounding.

To be lifted above the briar patch was the gift of this teaching. You don't have to go back into it. It is there if you want it. But the claim has been made, and the crucible of fear has been exposed as the lie that it is.

To be in an encounter with fear does not mean you have to be afraid. To be in an encounter with fear and remain unafraid is how you know you have lifted.

We thank you each for the claim you have made with us. The claim "I am free," the claim of liberation, the claim of being outside of the claims made for you or by the collective, the liberation you seek is here, is here, is here. And as we say these words, we will complete this chapter of this text.

Thank you each and good night. Stop now, please. Period. Period. Period.

Chapter Six

UNDOING THE KNOWN

Day Nine (Continued)

The thought of you as the True Self is confounding to you because you have no idea what it is to be made manifest beyond the agreements that you have made thus far. The totality of expression, the True Self in full expression, will be described herein as a state of being in identification with its Source, who perceives the Source of all things in what he or she perceives. That's a very simple declaration, but if you understood the magnitude of the meaning, it means you are no longer what you thought you were, nor is what you see, what you comprehend, what you engage with. The totality of your experience is transformed by the alignment you have attended to, and the manifestation of it, the congruence with the known in a new way, is what you attend to.

Now the requirements for change have been laid out before: the re-identification with the self in form and field, and then the alignment to it, which claims manifestation. The requirement of change makes itself known through the process of change, and rarely before. When you are in a wind, you might not know where you stand until the wind has ceased. Once you find out where you are, the requirements of the landscape that you are in make themselves known, and you may attend to them in that way.

The desire to know what happens next, what it seems to be or may look like, what it should be if you had your way, is what we must attend to now. With all conviction, you have decided that the world that you live in is the only world you may know, and the requirement of that is a limited expression on the physical plane. The idea of another world, or another octave, another way of being expressed, seems magical to you, perhaps attractive, perhaps foolish. But if we were to tell you that other worlds exist with you concurrent to the one that you are in, in this same shared space, but at different levels of vibration, you would be shocked, perhaps, at what that really means. It means that the delineation of a shared reality that you have entrusted yourself to has claimed you in a limited way at the cost of other things that may be known.

Imagine, if you wish, that you are in a great hall with many doorways. Each doorway has another experience to be understood beyond it, and each experience leads you to a different juncture, a different way of knowing the self. In fact, who you are exists in such a hallway and is opening every door. Each time she makes a choice, sets an intention, moves beyond the known, the next doors appear. We said doors, plural, because each choice magnifies its requirements as the door is opened, as the threshold is passed. You may choose one or the other, perhaps go from both to the next that appears down the hallway. The requirement for transformation will be met by you in each encounter as your soul is engaging with its requirements for development through each encounter you choose.

Now the requirement of realization is a bit different. As you are in the hallway and having these experiences in sequential ways that you understand in time, the unlimited self who expresses beyond time is also present and informing everything with its alignment. As you align to the divine mastery that we have been teaching you, how you choose is informed by this. What you choose and how you experience what you choose is also informed. This is why we say you have a very different experience as the True Self emerges in totality.

The expression of you at this level does not take you beyond the hallway, but the hallway itself is transformed, the hallway being the landscape you exist in, and the doors being the opportunities, the intentions set, the choices made, that contribute to your development that will bring you this way or that. The Divine as what you are in this hallway actually has access to different doorways operating in a higher way. She doesn't choose by knowing what she has known, she chooses by realizing what is present in the higher realm that she is beginning to attend to.

We will give you a very simple example for Paul, who is asking. Imagine that you live on a floor, an apartment building or a hotel. There are many doorways to different experiences, but all of these expressions exist on the same floor. If you go to a higher floor, the doorways will be there, but they will be in different expression, and higher still, and higher still. Opportunities do not cease, but what the Divine Self calls to her to realize herself through will be at a different level of engagement.

"How is this so?" he asks.

When you are operating in fear, you are immediately limited by the options you have. You will not attend to things that take you out of comfort unless you are thrust out or into a doorway that you wish you hadn't chosen. The Divine as what you are announces herself—"I am free, I am free, I am free"—and in that claim of freedom she realigns everything to a purview that does not agree to fear, and, consequently, what is chosen will be rather different.

The manifestation of choice, whatever that choice is, is

something you are accountable to. Each of you, independently, and the collective as a whole, has requirements that must be met, and you are responsible for every choice you make. At the higher level, the teaching doesn't cease. You must understand this. Some of you feel that, if you do all this work, or you align to the higher truth, you simply know everything all the time and your lessons cease. Why would this be so? Everything is always in motion, and your move toward realization—in increments, yes—toward fullness or totality, calls to you what you require even at the highest levels of embodiment.

If you can imagine that the beliefs that you hold as a small self are indeed limited, and you can't align to what you can't imagine or conceive of, you will understand this. Each of you chooses as best you can at the level of alignment you have agreed to based upon what you think you can have. Because the True Self is not limited in the same way, what becomes available—the different doorways, perhaps—will be very different. What is chosen by the True Self will always be to move the True Self into greater expression.

Now expression must be understood. The Divine as you in expression means who you are and how you be in expression as the what—not the idea of being—but being itself is expression. And, as you are expressed at the highest level that you can attend to, what you claim is of like accord. The manifestation of the Divine, in the individual, claims the Divine in manifestation in all the individual encounters. The collective, when rendered in truth, when the collective is known in truth, what the collective claims is a collective reality that does not aspire to the small doorways on the lower hall, but the high ones that can now be accessed because they have become available outside of limitation.

All limitation is, is an agreement to what can be at the cost of what you don't think is possible. In all of our teachings, we have told you that nothing can be claimed until it is first known as a possibility, and the requirement now, at this moment, is to accept the possibility that the manifestation of you in embodiment has access to far more than you have been permitted to know through the clarity or the injunction of a shared reality that says you are not allowed to move beyond what you have known.

Each of you comes in an awareness, already, that there is more to be claimed. But, still you list the "more" based on the lists that you have inherited—more abundance, better friendships, higher knowing. But even your prescription for these things is indoctrinated by the issuance of data and history. "What is higher knowing?" is still prescribed by you. "What is a better friend?" is still known by you through your idealization. You would never claim what you don't know or can't imagine. How possibly could you?

Each of you comes in a higher way to realize yourself

outside of the known, so what we wish to do with you now is lift you beyond the known to a new level of capacity to hold the potential that may be claimed. It must be understood that by doing this exercise, you are turning the page in a book to a book that has not yet been written. And if you do this, the pages must begin to fill with new possibilities, not the prescriptions of old, not the definitions you've used, which in and of themselves are limiting.

Each of you says yes to your potential only if it's going to give you what you think you want. You will not agree to a trip to an unknown place without knowing that there will be food and shelter awaiting you. You will not decide to take a step farther unless there is assurance that your comfort will not be met as it has been. And, as a result of this, very few of you go on the journey to full realization, because it requires the willingness to move beyond the known in absolute ways.

"What does that mean?" he asks. "Absolute ways?"

"It means to understand that each of you, in your claim of freedom, has been operating in a limited ideal of what freedom is. We will say this importantly. The claim of freedom breaks open the pages of the book and releases the definitions that you have utilized by inheritance to claim a reality in a limited dimensional place. What that means is, once you stop ascribing to what things should be, as they have been known, you can begin to experience what may be known that has yet gone unnamed. Do you understand this?"

Imagine that a book that could be read did not resemble what a book should look like. Imagine that the pages of the book did not resemble pages that you have seen before and the language on the page resembled no language that you have ever known. You will not read this book. You will decide it is not a book because it is not the known. This is the book we are offering you now. And if you hold yourself open to it, you may receive its wisdom.

But the agreement is a radical one. "I am willing to begin to experience my reality outside of history, definition, and collective agreement. I am willing to know the realities that coexist on this plane in higher octaves that may be understood or experienced for my benefit. I am willing to know beyond the known. I am willing to speak beyond language. I am willing to claim beyond intent. I am willing to see beyond perception. I am willing to claim the truth of vibration beyond any comprehension I may have had thus far. And in this claim I am awakened to the totality of the True Self that is known to me as the Divine what I am."

Here we go, friends, and here is the journey we offer you. Imagine that before you there is a text of the familiar, and there is one page to be turned. When the page is turned, the text opens to a void, and you may enter this void in the awareness that you are always safe in the True Self who is your companion here. By entering this void, this unknown space, you become the willing agreement of truth as can be expressed as what you are. And the qualities you require to be manifest as, for this to occur, are being emblazoned on your field in letters that you cannot read, but you can know the writing in the field is beyond language and full of intention for the causal field to be made manifest as flesh, the Divine as what.

Be still, and allow yourself to be emblazoned with the truth of your being. Be still, and allow the inscription of the Christed Self upon your field. Be still, and say yes, that what you will now encounter will be beyond what you can imagine, or could have assumed, or said yes to by the self who was informed in history.

Now the asking of this—"May I proceed?"—is essential. We want you each to go into your heart and ask this question of yourself: "May I proceed?" If the answer is yes, this book will remain open for you to experience in vibration. You will open the page, the blank page, to the void, and enter into it for your experience of content and knowing and experience. If you say no, we will hold the book handy for when your soul suggests you are prepared for this new encounter.

The obligation you have is to truth, not to us, and not to your ideas of what should be. The obligation you have is to the Divine, which is the essence of your entirety, and not to what you think it should look like. The Divine Self is afire as you, a blaze of brightness that cannot be seen by the mortal eye, but is lit on fire and perceived in fullness by those of us who attend to you in love. The truth of your being is brighter than you can see, has laughter and joy and fullness beyond what you can conceive of, and your requirement now is to say, "Yes, I may," if you choose. "Yes, I may know. Yes, I may be led to the high hallway with the beautiful doorway at the end that leads to all manifestation of God." Period. Period. Period. Period. Stop now, please.

(Pause)

If you each decide today that the what that you are is the manifestation of the Divine and can be nothing else, your time with us will have been very worthwhile. If each of you decides today that the comfort of the known may be released to a great adventure in being, your time with us will have been well spent. If each of you claims your potential, the realization of truth as who and what you are, each day for a moment or two at least, you will begin to comprehend that the eternal self, embodied as you, may be known, and claimed, and revealed as what you are in expression.

We will have to say a few things for Paul about the instruction that has been received because he is insistent in his questions. "What are the hieroglyphics? What do they mean?"

The imprinting in the field in the higher octave is done by us so that the field itself may support the alignment to Christendom, to the True Self in agreement that may be known by each of you. The field itself, in some ways, is a vortex for universal energy, and when the encoding is done in the field, the field itself is emblazoned to reinforce what the encoding requires.

The Divine Self in form and field, while it is what you are and have always been, has not been realized in fruition. And this is the work we do. The agreement you make, each of you who attends to these words, is that you will know who you are outside of the field that has claimed you thus far. The field that has claimed you thus far is a collective agreement of vibratory accord, a collective field.

Imagine, if you wish, a field, a great field, a landscape populated by beings agreeing to be in a shared construct for the purpose of learning, and for realization. As individuals in this field begin to move beyond the known, in fact they create the agreement for a new field to be built, or to be known, that exists in a new way. This cannot happen in the old, but the lifting to the new is what makes this so.

Once the new field is established or agreed to by enough

of you, it is available to all. It exists concurrently with the old until the new assumes it. Look at the passage of the Divine Self from the small self to full incarnation. We will give you an example. The small self's will, while active, may exist concurrently with the will of the True Self. But as the braiding occurs, the will of the small and the True, finally the will of the small is known only in the new way. It has become assumed by the new.

You can realize your own passage this way. As the small self is assumed by the True Self, you can understand that the collective small self, or agreement to this plane in limited ways, may be assumed by the higher, that higher hallway we referenced earlier, which exists concurrently to the hallway on the lower floor. As enough of you decide to be what you are—and this decision is not made by the small self, although the small self must agree to it in order for the will to be braided and the coalescence to occur in vibration—the agreement is made to be made manifest at a level of vibration that you can all align to.

Imagine that field again, that wonderful field with so many beings in it, now existing in a higher way. What was known in history, the way we were, the way things used to be, will be accepted as what it was, a construct made in lower vibration that you have surpassed and evolved beyond. Let's look at the word *evolved*. You evolve beyond the known to the unknown, and in the unknown the new may be claimed. The new is never claimed within the known. Do you understand this? So as the unknown is placed before you, as you enter the void of the unknown, you are agreeing to learn and to access the wisdom that does not exist in the lower field. You are actually claiming access to the divinity and the agreement to be in manifestation that has precluded you in the lower field because the collective had said no, or been fearful, or been told it could not be.

Now, as we teach you each in the ways you may learn, we also must address the collective. Everybody who hears these words has a community that they reside in, people that they encounter every day. As the echo of the resonance of your field is in encounters with others, the emblazoning in the field that you have been attended to by actually sings and claims itself in what you see, and in who you see as well. By very definition of your being, your world is reclaimed by your presence within it. Now by *reclaimed* we mean re-known in a higher way. By reclaimed we mean re-seen in a higher way that could not have been attended to through the perspective, or ideology, or agreements made in the lower field.

This is transition. It's as if you are moving to a higher octave—as you get used to the higher field, it is quite comfortable. It is the transition, always, from the familiar to the unknown that requires a reckoning, and a reckoning, as we say, a facing of the self and its creations, will be encountered by all of you as you move beyond what you've known and decide you no longer require what you thought you did to be who you thought you were. Underline the word *thought*. It is just a thought. It is just a thought that you need to be a certain way, look a certain way, have a certain profession or ideology. What else could it be? It is a thought that you have made so.

As you release the thought, the manifestations of that thought may be known and said yes to, or no to, depending on their merit. We will give you an example. You have a winter coat in the closet. You live in a tropical climate. Do you require the winter coat or do you let it go? You have a winter coat in the closet. You live in a tundra. Not a bad idea to hold on to that coat. It is still useful for your requirements. These things will be made known to you, individually or collectively, as part of the transition that you will undergo.

We sing your song for you until you know the words. When we say we know who you are, we know who you are outside of what you think, and we will not embarrass you by saying what you think you are, because what you think you are is far less than you could ever be in truth. The True Self as what, the Divine as what, the claim of being—"I am free"—is what we are here for you with. And your agreement to be with us is being met in all ways with a comprehension of your individual requirements for transformation.

One size does not fit all, and what she requires to align herself in a higher way may be very different than him. And, as we say yes to the transition that you are undertaking, we also must say that the claim of truth—"I am free, I am free, I am free"—when invoked, will support you from the myriad of issues that will be seen by you as seeking to contain you, or to reinforce the known that is seeking to be released by you.

This is not about drastic action. This is not about being foolhardy. This is about being present for what occurs, what will be known by you as your growth proceeds. And by *growth*, we mean your evolution.

We will say thank you now for your attention to these words. This is in the text, yes, and we will say thank you. Period. Period. Period. Stop now, please.

Day Ten

Trust yourselves, please, to require yourself to call to you what you need. Trust yourselves, please, to be in charge, in some ways, of the emotional self that would seek to claim you in times of uncertainty. Trust yourself, please, that the Divine as what you are seeks its recognition in the life you live in ways that are palpable to you that can be known and understood. Ask yourself, if you wish, if you are willing to know beyond the known. Are you willing to claim beyond what has been taught to you? Are you willing to become an emissary to a new logic that exists in a higher way than you have been instructed in prior?

"A new logic," you say. "What does that mean?"

It means that the identity you hold that has been so informed by teachings and ramifications of teachings, encounters with your lives and the lives of those who've lived before, you have understood yourself in very small ways. The testament of another becomes your reality, and an agreed upon reality that you all partake in, a collective reality. "This is the air and the sky." "This is the earth and the rain." "This is how we know one another." All of these things, in some ways, have been prescribed to you, and your relationships to them are informed by the history that you continue to claim to it.

What if there was another way? What if there was another ideal? What if there was another way of being in response to a reality without the codification, even the language that has been utilized by you each to confirm what you see? Understand this idea. You confirm everything you see by the names it is given. "That is a house." "That is a pool." "That is a woman." "That is an airplane." You understand things that are perceived by you through how you have been taught to identify them.

"Well, what is wrong with that?" he asks. "Why would that be wrong?"

It is not wrong in the least, but it is only one way to be in perception of a world. The qualification that we seek to bring to you is that the language that you exist in is participatory, and the fabric of language, if you can understand it, is made into form by the dedication to the belief that what you see is what it is supposed to be. "I know what a chair looks like. This will be a chair." "I know what a sky is. This will be a sky."

Now there is a sky, yes, and the man before you sits in a chair, but the landscape he exists in is far greater than what you are perceiving him in, or he is knowing himself in. The landscape and the fabric of his reality is operating in multiple octaves, and you are witnessing only the ones that you are in coherence to, and the names you give things in all ways solidify your experience and claim it for you. The divine potential that you each have exceeds the known, exceeds the language that you have utilized to describe it. All language, we suggest, operates in limitation, because the ideas behind language have done their best. To be claimed in these ways does not mean that the ideas themselves can't exist beyond them. The ideas do exist beyond the known. The ideas do exist even beyond language.

Now all things are ideas. The chair is an idea. The house

is an idea. The airplane is an idea that has been claimed in form, and, if you really wish to know, the sky is an idea as well, as is the sea, as is the earth. Everything is first idea, then made form through consequence and attention and the idealization of language. You have heard of names claiming things into being. "This will be a horse." "That will be a serpent." And the names things have been given have claimed form, and you have idealized these forms and repeated them throughout time. You know what a horse will be, what a landscape should look like. The ideas that have become things were taken from a large field and made manifest, and the un-manifest is where we seek to take you and are inviting you to come to—the un-manifest, the potential of the Divine to be known beyond logic and limitation.

The acquisition of your inheritance as a divine being can be limited by what you believe you can receive. The alignment you require to lift beyond the known to the triumph of the new, to the gift of the new that you may align as, is being brought to you in this text as you agree to it. The vibrations you hold, in some ways, are already accessing the limited, and as you move beyond them, you access the infinite. So your progress has to become from the known to the implicit. What is implicit is within and exists beyond the known.

The implicit nature of the human being is not his gender or his character. It's the form itself that you know itself as, the form itself that may be named as a being. The further names you give things—"this is a man, his name is Fred, he has an occupation"—are further ways of limiting and delineating what the man is. But, finally, the idea of the man, of the human, is the form it has taken.

To move beyond the form is to realize what is implicit in the form. The Divine is implicit in all manifestation because nothing exists without it or outside of it. So as the man is seen as the field beyond the gender, beyond the functions of the body, it begins to align to its true potential to be manifest as the True Self. The True Self will not be limited by the organs of the body, or the shade of the skin, or even the temperament of the being himself. The Divine as you, once remade in a new alignment, moves beyond the known as a system—underline *system*—the Divine as a system operating as you.

You have always been a conduit of function. You know what you do. You use the facilities, you feed the body, you take care of yourself as you can, and the system itself agrees to be taken care of, and this is the manifestation you've known yourself as. As we teach you, we teach you that the higher system is the divine expression that seeks to operate as you—underline *as*—and be realized through you. And the function of the system as an operative of the Divine is you become the conduit of it, and the expression of it, and the knowing of it, all at once. The being, expression, and knowing of the Divine all at one moment.

How this happens, as we suggest, in sequence, is through the release of the acquisitions that the small self has known and identified through, and then the collective expressions that have bound humanity in limitation. The function of this teaching is the realization of the True Self in expression. "I know how I serve." And the realization of this requires the alignment to lift beyond all prescription, and even the limitations of language, to align itself to a consummate truth. All are one. That is the consummate truth. All are one.

In this realization, the echo of your field becomes a transmitter of the Divine in its expression for the sake of all. As you have moved beyond limitation to freedom, and beyond fear as a way of knowing the self in interactions with the self and others, you make the new agreement that what may be known in form may have been prior unknown.

Here we go, friends:

"I am accepting myself as released from all barriers made by language in limitation to access the truth of who I am as may be known as the infinite truth that seeks to know me as who and what I am. And, as I say these words, I am permitting myself to trust this passage to the higher realm, where I may be readdressed as the what that I am in agreement to serve. I know who I am in truth. I know what I am in truth. I know how I serve in truth. I am free. I am free. I am free."

Now ask yourself this: Are you willing to die to the life that you have known? What is a death, but a transition? Are you willing to release the idealization of the life that you think you should live? All an idealization is, is a supposition, and expectation of a possibility. Are you willing to release the necessary things that would support you in making this passage in joy, beyond fear, and the requirements that fear would bring you? To die to the old is to be born anew, and the passage to the Kingdom, the awareness of the presence of the Divine in all things, manifests this way as the skin is shed, as the cocoon is released, as the body itself accepts its role as a system of agreement for the expression of God, or what you would call God as.

The significance of this teaching tonight is that it will lift you beyond the claims you've made in identity to the unknown where the self may be revealed. The Divine as what you are must be revealed to you beyond what you think it is, or think it should be, for it to be known in fullness. And the gift of this is the release of the self, and the alignment of the self to the new that will claim it in love and in freedom for all to know.

"What is this teaching?" he asks. "Is this freedom from fear?"

It is the release of fear by the being of the new, and the acquiescence to what exists beyond the systems of logic that you have utilized to support yourselves in a limited expression. You all know that two plus two equals four, and as you agree to this, you limit the possibilities of another arithmetic that may exist in some other way. Everything that has been settled upon, as all and what it was, will now have to be re-known by the self who is willing to express herself beyond the systems that she has inherited. And this will not be done by the language and the manifestations that language has made into form without the cleaning of the slate.

"What is the cleaning of the slate?" he asks.

If you were to spell a word, you can understand that the letters that comprise the word can be reordered and made something new. This is the way we operate. You are not negated as you lift beyond the known. You are re-experienced and reclaimed and remade in a new octave while you inhabit and manifest in the collective field that you have all embodied in. As the collective field is made manifest in your presence, the field itself begins to lift in octaves to meet where you stand.

If you can imagine that your very presence on the lawn lifts the flowers to your height, you would have an example of what the field does when it oscillates in the high light that is the Christed Self. What is made manifest may be re-known, the letters reordered or reclaimed to summon a new response. The idealization of what was has been dismantled enough, at this juncture in time, that your agreement that there may be something new to be claimed has become present. The vase, in some way, has a crack in it, and that crack is an opportunity to re-understand what a vase must be, and what now may be made in a new way.

This is a gift, you see. But the breaking of the vase, the re-rendering of the old to participate in change, is very challenging to the small self, whose designs are in agreement to what has been. "Behold, I make all things new" is an alignment to a higher frequency, and what is perceived at this frequency may exist beyond what has been understood and given language to prior. When you lift in octaves, you begin to access information and knowing that has existed, but not been available to you through the veils or the density of your material existence. So this is cause for celebration, but also for the requirements of manifestation to be made known to you so you can consummate this agreement by your agreement to be what you are.

Now the divine marriage, the Divine as what, the implicit taking of form, the implicit being in expression of the Divine as what, has always been this teaching. It has never been comfortable to the attitude of the small self, nor has it ever been convenient to the cultural dictates that you find yourself living in and agreeing to each day. "What will I be? How do I manage? What do I become?" says the small self in the face of a storm. "What will I be? How will I know myself? What will be guaranteed to me?" announces the small self, as she faces destiny that is unprescribed.

"Undoing the Known" would be the title of this chapter, as if you are unfurling a sweater that has been made, so that it may be re-knit in some other form, and that is the passage you are in now, not only as a being, but as a species. The unraveling simply renders the old in a new way, and a new form will then be taken that is the requirement of the times one stands in. See this passage in its potential. See this passage as meritful. See this passage as a new allowance to claim what exists beyond what has been in form—that which has no name, that which will be surrendered to, that which will be loved and known as Source, or the Divine, that is the stars, and the sky, and the breath, and the sight, and death itself. All is of, or nothing is.

The passage that you undergo individually claims the new for you. By nature of undergoing the passage, you have to claim the new. It is the result of the birth that you be born. It is the result of the passage that you are reclaimed. And while this is done at the level of the microcosm, at the small self's level, it is also being done in a large way as each human being on this plane is being seen and re-known beyond the contributions that she has endowed herself with as a small self.

Each human being, each speck of the Divine in its illumination, makes a great blaze. And the world, we suggest, is soon to be afire with this light as humanity itself makes the decision that it will live, it will survive, it will reclaim itself beyond fear, beyond separation, and beyond the limitation that you have utilized to keep yourself in separation from the Divine and one another. Period. Period. Period.

Q: I know we have all these incantations that we can say verbally, or we can say them in our mind. I'm curious if there's any effective difference between saying them verbally or in our mind and what would that be?

A: Yes and no. They will work silently very effectively. When they are intoned aloud, the resonance of the voice will support the field itself in its recognition of the speech you have made. Imagine the sound of a gong that echoes around the room. Everything in the room is in response to the gong. When you claim "I know who I am, I know what I am, I know how I serve," this is the vibration that informs the field. In this case, yes, thinking it will work. But the intention behind the thought needs to be true. These are not wishful thinking phraseologies. They are intonations and claims of truth. When you claim it as what it is—what is true is always true—you will meet the benefit of it. Period. Period. Period.

Q: I have an adopted little girl who was very fearful from the day she was born. Do the Guides have any advice on how to deal with the fear of young children?

A: There is a need for calming and soothing, but supporting courage, which is not agreeing to fear, will last her in a longer stead than a pat on the head and a hug. She needs to understand that when the lights are out, things have not moved around. She needs to understand that, when you are not present, you are still somewhere. She needs to be told that, if she is fearful, she has another option, another way to think, that is always available to her, and that she has the power to choose that. Period. Period. Period.

Ask each one present to know themselves as safe. Sit where you are and know that you are safe, just as you are. Whatever your expectations may have been for this exchange, they were rendered by the small self. Whatever activations you've received have been the gift of the True Self, who is the true recipient of these teachings and will lift you with them in her agreement to be known. As we see you each, we see you beyond fear, the prescriptions of fear, and the idolization of fear that is prominent on this plane now. When fear is an idol, it is your god. Do not pray to fear. It is a liar. We thank you each, and we love you each as we know who you are, what you are, and how you serve. Blessings and goodnight. Stop now.

Day Eleven

Resolve yourselves today to dismantle the structures that would impede you from realization through adherence to this teaching, through reliance upon the Divine Self and not the small will to respond to the requirements of transformation. The key to change, we would suggest, at this time, is reliance upon truth and the Divine Self to contend with all distortion that would present itself to keep you where you have been. There is not a tug-of-war, per se, Paul, who is asking from the background. There is a new reliance that is needed on the Divine Self to withstand an encounter with fear or choose to lift above fear when it presents itself.

Humanity itself is at a juncture now, and the reliance upon the old to solve your difficulties will not serve you in the ways that you hope it would. Reliance upon truth and the Divine within all things will give you the actions you require in the physical realm to withstand all change. When change comes, it may come quietly, or with thunder. It really matters not. The aspect of you that will withstand all change is the True Self, and your reliance upon her to give you ballast in the storm, to support you in change, will be the key to liberation from the net of fear that would seek to capture you within it.

When humanity is transitioning, one and all, to a new level of being, the cauterization of fear must be understood as a requirement. To cut yourself off from fear only means you do not rely upon it to serve you or protect you. Instead, you rely upon truth and divinity, the light that you are, to illumine the darkness and show you the right way forward.

Paul is seeing an image of many people running in mazes, torches high, seeking to find their way out. You will not find yourself out of the maze of fear by diving through it, but by lifting above it. That is why we say truth, which is a higher frequency than fear, and by love, which will show you that you are protected from transformation when you become frightened of the prospect of it.

What if each human being were standing in a doorway to a new life? What if every man born was standing in the hallway of a new passage? We will tell you this. This is where you stand, and the agreements made in fear throughout time would seek to tease you, to invite you back to them to the promise of the known and the encounters of safety that are born in deceit. What is a promise of safety born in deceit? It is better to be in the pain that you are in, in the shadows that you stand in, than to venture out of them. It is better to lie and pretend your complacency is productive, when in truth it is not. It is better to achieve for selfish reasons than to rely upon the True Self to use you well for the benefit of all. The safety of the known, the acquiesced to, the structural norms that you have used to verify your experience here—the journey forward, as we have said, comes at the cost of the old.

But you must understand, friends, this is not about being noble and agreeing to change. It is about realizing that the change is inevitable. So how you are carried through it, in every way, is dependent upon your reliance of truth and the realization that you are free. In freedom, you are announced, one and all, at the inception of your soul. The realization of this has been the passage for many of you through lifetimes of ignorance or fear. The realization that the True Self as what you are is made manifest now by agreeing to it, aligning to it, and aligning to its manifestation and realization is the simple passage you are in an encounter with. Divinity itself, in an abstract way, means next to nothing to you. But your comprehension of your true nature as of your Source may support you more readily in your comprehension of what realization is. The true as what in manifestation is the key to being at this level of agreement and manifestation.

Now why do we speak of the world this way? Why do we speak of the times this way? Because you have chosen collectively to move beyond the known, and the passage forward, in some ways, is fraught with danger, but danger to the small self, not to the True Self, because the True Self realizes the benefits of mass change even when the small self cannot.

"But isn't there change that is not productive?" Paul is asking. "Aren't there reasons to fear dictatorships or fear change that is enforced upon us?"

In fact, the action of fear is to reproduce itself, so there is no need to fear, and perhaps not all change is of high vibration. You may leave a house by walking out the front door, or burning it down around you. Do you understand this? Please walk through the front door whenever possible. But those of you who refuse to transform may choose to burn the house down around you so that the change itself is the inevitable product of choice, and collective choice, we suggest, not to change, which will bless you anyway with the changes you require.

When something is destroyed, it can be made new. When something is abandoned, it can be responded to in a rather different way. "We have outgrown the need for this, we may learn in other ways. We are not damning ourselves by damning our past creations. We are lifting above them in a collective agreement that we may know ourselves and our fellows in a higher way."

The times you stand in, we suggest, have been agreed upon by the collective. You can no longer go down a road of self-destruction or collective destruction without realizing the futility of it. As this is realized, you are awakening to what options you can claim, and some of you are realizing that to be in battle with anything is to claim yourself at war and align to the very things that you say you do not want. So the process of lifting in vibration, or ascension, has been claimed by humanity as the opportunity for its progress and its receipt of its true inheritance.

This has always been your purview. You must understand this. It has always been the requirement of the soul to realize itself in fullness. The collective agreement to become manifest in a higher octave at the cost of what has been is a new idea only to some of you. The realization of truth was prescribed for you in every religion humanity has claimed, but has been greatly distorted throughout the ages. So the mystic may realize herself, but the common man cannot.

The inherent choice to realize the self now is not done for the singular, but for the collective, and some of you will not like this. You are not doing this for yourselves in the ways that you may think. You may be doing this for two generations behind you, who will know you by the work you have gifted them with—you, all of you, who have claimed "Yes, I know who I am, I know what I am, I know how I serve, I am free, I am free, I am free."

Each of you comes to us with an awareness of your requirements for evolution. And humanity itself, every culture on this globe, claims the same. If you can imagine this, the collective energy of a country and its own karma, its own lessons and requirements for growth are being attended to concurrently with the individuals. Everything is in transition. The planet itself, in its adherence to reality as you have claimed it, is also in ambition to transform because you have chosen in your own ways to decide that your survival was not dependent upon the globe itself. As that is transitioning, so is your relationship to the very earth that you stand upon.

So if you can understand that everything changes, none of it is necessarily terribly comfortable, you can also understand that those things that you would avoid or seek to dismantle to get your own way may be providing you or humanity with the very encounter you need to realize the Divine, or the holy, or the truth in all manifestation. It is very difficult to look away when you see a crime against humanity, and you can realize yourself as participant to the creation and move in action, or move in consciousness, to challenge, or reclaim, or re-create any manifestation of consciousness that you are in an encounter with. To assume that your presence at a war is negligible is to make yourself complicit to the war itself. You are complicit to war because you witness it, and, as you lift above it, you may realize it in the higher octave and lift all things that would be known in war to a level of recognition where war cannot be.

"How is this done?" he asks.

By witness, yes, but also by realization. To realize the Divine in the self is to realize the Divine in what you witness, and by this realization you cannot condemn, because to condemn denies the light that is implicit in all. To realize something is to lift it.

"But if we expose a fear, if we expose a lie, aren't we lifting it in a different way?"

Yes, in fact, you are. When we said you manage the storm before you by aligning to truth, it also includes the ability to speak it. But to speak the truth does not make others wrong. To speak the truth is to announce what is, not to condemn the liar, but to expose the lie, and you understand the difference here, yes. To expose the lie is to bring it to light. The liar himself is accountable to his choice and will reap the benefits of whatever actions he has taken, high, or low, or in-between.

You must know that the individual is accountable to all of his actions. So is a culture. So is a country. And the collective itself must realize itself as the liar it has been when it has decided to rule by war, or by control, or by subservience to a lower ideal.

Each of you comes with witness to history. Understand and agree to that. You have known yourselves in history. It is time to know yourselves as free from the very things that you have used to dictate what your reality should be based upon what it was. As we continue this text, we intend to realize the reader, not only as complicit to his exchange with his reality, but liberated from that as the one who may know himself anew. And the alignment you require to transition from one state of consciousness to the higher that is present here will be offered to you in love and in agreement to your capacity to receive and know it, and, yes, by *know* we mean realize it.

Ask yourself this question now: "Am I willing to know who and what I am and express it in higher ways? Am I willing to say yes to this passage through change so that I may support others in their awareness of truth? Am I willing to sing the song of truth, the song of freedom in the face of what would counter me? And am I willing to say yes to who and what I am when I would be denied by my fellows, or my world?"

If you are willing, we will take your hands now, and we

will say this is the end of this chapter. Thank you for your patience and your attendance to these words. Period. Period. Period. Stop now, please.

(Pause)

Questions on the teaching, if you wish.

Q: How do we take full responsibility for our complicity in history and in lies in the past?

A: What a wonderful question. The first thing is to accept that you have been complicit, and, in fact, are, simply by nature of being. This does not require penance. It simply requires acknowledgment. You cannot look at a fountain without being in relationship to the fountain. If the fountain is spurting blood, you are in a foundation of congruence with that. To realize your complicit nature in anything you see is simply to acknowledge yourself at a vibratory frequency where this expression can be met. How you move beyond it is through the instructions we have given you. First a realization of self: "I know who I am, I know what I am, I know how I serve, I am free, I am free, I am free." And then the realization of what you see as the True Self perceives it.

What you end up doing instead is going into an agreement with historical data. "This is what this fountain is," and, consequently, what it means. You claim the inheritance that you have been given in narrative to know something in the language that it was used as a descriptor for. To move beyond it, again, is to rise above it through the alignment you can hold. How the Divine Self witnesses another is very different than how the small self would. When the Divine Self comes forth in witness to anything, it elevates the thing that is seen and responded to. Period. Period. Period.

Q: What does it feel like to witness something in truth as one who has risen above?

A: The realization of it in a higher way is not about what it feels like, but what it is. To codify it with emotion is then to seek to grab the historical information. "This should feel joyful." "This should feel terrible." To witness anything in the higher octave is to receive it as it truly is without the emotion attached, but the agreement to its being. This isn't about fixing things. It's about realizing them. Do you understand the difference here? Somebody is wounded. "What a terrible thing," you say. "How could this have happened?" Again, the small self is deciding what is, based on a narrative of what should or should not be. The True Self realizes the suffering of the one who is wounded, may tend to it, but in some ways the event itself is neutral, does not carry with it the distortion of history.

The reliance upon the old to remedy a situation is usually by provocation. Do you understand this? "Look at that terrible event. We will fight it together." And, in that act, you become complicit to war. To realize the act itself as a way of being expressed, know who you are and then witness the event in a higher way. Realizing the Divine that is expressing in ways you could not have seen as the small self in fact transforms your relationship to it. The Divine witnesses the Divine in what it sees. Do you understand this? It places nothing outside of God, so it can't condemn in the way the small self would. But do you attend to the man's wound who is bleeding? Of course you do. You do it with love and compassion. You even love the one who wounded the man because you know who he is as well.

You do not deny God when you don't get what you want. Do you understand this? That is the convenience of the old. "Where was God there? There can be no God." The implicit nature of the Divine in all manifestation is what is realized by the one who knows who she is, and that transforms the landscape, because what you witness in the higher octave must lift to meet you. Period. Period. Period.

Q: I understood the Guides said that our work would take one or two generations to be of benefit, so . . .

A: Not necessarily. But that is what you fear. The benefit at a global level of the manifestation of the Divine Self, which is being imprinted now for realization, may not align in fullness in the lifetime you express in. That doesn't mean you don't know it or experience it. We are speaking manifestation. When you understand that the collective itself is claiming manifestation and much of the turmoil you see is about the transformation of the identity of this plane—"Who are we to one another? Will we survive what we have claimed? Will we live beyond what we've known?"—these are all ways of announcing potential—do you understand this?—a new potential, not a dire reality. But when faced with a potential reality that you wish to say no to, you seek something higher. You have not been put in this position as a culture in this country for some time. You have been very patient with getting your needs met as you think they will be, and, in some ways, now that you are not, you are saying, "Hey, wait a minute. What is happening here?" What is happening here is that you are no longer asleep and you are finding yourselves awakening in a very uncomfortable bed that you thought was made of feather and down. Do you understand this, yes? Period. Period. Period.

Q: In our knowing ourselves as Divine and seeing the Divine in what we see around us, is it enough to do this in just our

everyday life, and, as you've often taught us, to attend to
someone in front of us in pain, but should this also take some
kind of action, social action, in the world? Is it enough to be
at home in my own comfortable life seeing the world to the
best of my capacity as the Divine?

A: It depends on who you are and how you serve. This is
individualized. The claim "I know how I serve" is made by
the True Self, and if the True Self needs action she will claim
it. She will not be able to say no to it. She will be out where it
matters, claiming the divinity or the truth in what she sees.
Perhaps you may go out. Perhaps you may stay in. And what
your work would be, would be holding the world in a higher
way. There isn't one way that this teaching is applied, because the action of the True Self as expressed by you will be
what moves you forward. Period. Period. Period.

Q: Is there like a tipping point where enough people, like 25
percent or 30 percent of the country, would have to witness
in a higher way for the country to actually shift?

A: That's not the way it works, although the mathemati-
cians would perhaps say it does. Consciousness expressed by
the individual does not operate individually, but informs the
collective. Do you understand this? You are not in a silo in

your expression. Your expression, in fact, is contributing to the manifestation of the reality that you are seeing right now. Your presence in this room, wherever you hear these words, is claiming these words as a reality that you are experiencing. The very nature of your being in consort with your fellows supports the reality that you share. The idea of a tipping point is mostly understood as critical mass. When enough people get fed up with the menu at the restaurant, they will demand a better menu or go eat elsewhere. When the bulk of you realize that damning your fellows claims you in fear, perhaps you will change your minds. But in fact what happens is that some of you realize yourself and pave the way for those who follow.

We have used the example in prior texts of one with a machete clearing away the underbrush on the path before her. She has laid a path by nature of the fact that she walked it. Your agreement to be in this encounter is actually serving those who will come behind you, because the energy of this expression and this transmission itself will echo beyond these walls. Once a word is spoken, the word has always been spoken and may be heard in other octaves through an infinity. You don't understand this because you perceive time in a very linear way. The echo of a sound is existing throughout time. The wings of the butterfly are flapping throughout time. Everything is in an encounter with the manifest and the unmanifest. When enough of you realize yourselves, you have the conversation that perhaps can be had in a very different way about what it means to be with one another. And that is a conversation, we suggest, that is already beginning to happen.

"How does humanity align to a new way of being? How do we survive our tendency to war? How do we agree to what freedom is in a way that may be understood by all of humanity?" The designs that you have inherited that realize separation are what are being attended to now. And your agreement to separation as a manifest thing—"Because it has been, it will always be"—will be understood by you as something that you've known and can move beyond. Period. Period. Period.

Q: I'm very interested in the concept of healing across time. Lately I've been very attracted to reading historical fiction set in World War II, and to watching movies focused on the Holocaust. I feel within myself that there is a healing of that period of history, because, whenever I see the atrocities I Word through them. It's very easy for me to Word through those that my personality would call victims, it's much more difficult for me to Word through the so-called perpetrators and see them with the eyes of the Christ, but I feel that healing is going on inside of me and I'm wondering, it doesn't seem like it would stop with me, it feels like somehow that's a benefit to the present situation in the world and I'm wondering whether I understand that correctly.

A: Yes and no. Your realization of the divinity in those who came before you does transcend time because the Divine was as present then as it is now, so again you are claiming what is always true. Do you understand this? When you claim the Divine in another, you are not blessing their behavior or their role in a situation. You are claiming the aspect of them that is present always, and your realization of this does exist beyond what you know of as time because the Divine Self exists beyond time, but may be known in time. So you are contributing to healing, yes.

Are you transforming history? In fact you are transforming your relationship to it, and to the extent that you can realize the truth in the ones who are harmed in the war, you are supporting healing them as well. How could you not? If prayer only existed in a linear time, it would be fruitless. Do you understand this? Now, what prayer is, as you are working with it, is the realization of the Divine in matter that is present always, regardless of appearance or circumstance. We must say, though, to lift others to truth means moving them beyond how even history has emblemized them. Do you understand this? There is a polarity here. In any exchange or in any encounter, there are reasons and lessons for all who are involved. Do you understand this? So to separate the victim from the perpetrator is to deny the perpetrator his own divinity, which will also heal him and his complicitness to the encounter.

All manifestation is agreed upon. You wake up every morning. You see the sky. You agree to the sky. You see an atrocity. You claim it an atrocity and you have decided your relationship to it. To lift that thing to a higher octave is to reveal yourself as present as formless in the face of something else that may be known in a different way. To codify reality—"This is a teacup, that is a chair, it will always be a teacup, it will always be a chair"—is to claim that reality itself cannot know itself in a transformed way. The moment the teacup is broken, it can be called something else. When the legs of the chair are put into the fire, they are known as something else. Your relationship to everything may be altered when you stop deciding what something is through historical prescription. Now this is for Paul. We are not denying what happened. We are speaking about realizing it in a very different way, and there is a difference between the two. Period. Period. Period.

Chapter Seven

REVELATION

Day Twelve

When you come to us in your own authority—"I am willing to change"—you are met by us in agreement. We know
who you are. We know your capacity for change. And great
change may come to the one who is willing to be met in
truth. Underline this. *To be met in truth* means that you are
willing to be encountered with all aspects of yourself available to be witnessed. You don't hide something in shame.
You don't pretend that something didn't happen to move beyond it. You align to the True Self, the magnificent True
Self, who is whole, and holy, yes, and healed. And you announce yourself as fully available to an encounter with it. "I
am fully available to an encounter with my True Self to be
known in a higher way."

Now we will explain *higher way*. The density of the field that you know yourself through, the claims you have made to encourage fear, the denial of the self that you have utilized as a defense over the years, has claimed you in density, individually, yes, collectively, yes. The encounter with the higher, to be known in a higher way, is to be expressed and realized in a higher way, and this will happen—underline *will*—when all aspects of the self are revealed to the Divine Self to be known and realized in a higher way. The damage that was done to you as a child, the guilt you feel over harm done to another, the tragedies of the past, those things you will never get over, the rectitude, the solitude, the self-damnation, whatever it may be, are not insurmountable, but must be recognized and aligned to in a higher way.

Now do you need to go through your life and look at every incident and reveal yourself in this fashion? Not really. You may, if you wish, and you will reap benefits from that. Every memory, every idea, every thought born in fear, born in anger, born in shame, when offered to the light, may be seen and known in a higher octave and healed, if you wish, although we prefer the term *revealed*, in a higher way—a revelation, a new idea that replaces the old that is not a thought of condemnation or fear or shame or self-abasement. The True Self is not capable of those things. Do you understand this, friends? The True Self is not capable of self-abasement or anger or fear. She may know righteous action. She may know incredulity at the folly of humanity. But she knows it in compassion, as well. She does not damn another. She lifts another up to be seen in a higher way to be revealed. This is the chapter of Revelation and we are welcoming you to it now. To be revealed in a higher octave is to be in an encounter with the higher vibration.

When something has been hidden from the light, put away or put aside, the light cannot shine upon it. The retrieval of the old may be done in two ways—by offering, or release that is justified or responded to by incident. We will explain this for Paul. You may say, "Take this from me," or you may be hiding it behind your back and it may be revealed of its own action. When someone awakens to a behavior that is limiting them, it usually comes at a cost. How many of you would take advantage of another, knowing the cost of it? But most of you don't know how and when you take advantage. You have been doing your best, and in many ways you have been complicit to actions that you were told you were justified in by the cultures you inhabit. "It is all right to lie a little if you don't hurt their feelings." "It is all right to say these things about those people because we have the right to say them." "I am not antagonizing the whole by calling them a name. I am just showing you how wise I am."

You will never heal your world by damning anyone. You may heal them by exposing them to truth, or revealing them for what they are or what they do. Now the depth of the what they are must be comprehended by you. He is a man. He tells tall tales. We know he tells tall tales. We claim him as a liar and we stop there. He is a liar because he acts in lies, but the lies are born in fear, and the action of fear upon him is claiming everything he encounters. So to reveal him as free of fear, to know him as he may be known, the Divine Self that expresses as him that is fraught with lies, entangled by the weeds of them, may liberate the man because the lies will not exist in the higher octave.

Now the man that we call the tall tale teller is enjoying his lies or trusts lies to keep him safe. He relies upon the ways he has known himself to protect himself and what he believes to be important. He will not reveal himself in the first way we suggested. "Dear Lord, take my lies from me." He will be seen as the liar or exposed by the action of the lie. He may be redeemed by either action, and all we mean by *redeemed* is revealed at a higher way to be who and what he is in truth. The moment you decide that a man may never change, will never change, you have turned your back upon him. The moment you turn to face him, and claim him in truth, and realize the liberation of his soul that is his birthright, you may announce him in the higher field and he may be lifted to it. "You are free, you are free, you are free" is a claim of truth. You are not telling him he is free of the lies. It is implicit in the claim that the Divine in him can be revealed.

Paul says, "'Can'? Why not 'will'?"

Because the human being has will himself, and the acquiescence to the higher will, perhaps supplication—"Take this from me, I cannot abide the lies"—may be met in truth. But the small self's will has a deep desire to maintain its purview, its landscape, that he believes will get him what he requires to manifest the small man's kingdom. The small man's kingdom is ever present. Look around you. Look at the systems you've agreed to. Look who has the funds, who desires the funds, who thinks they are better than the ones beside them because they have more money or beauty or ambition. You understand this. You live in this world, and in fact are complicit to it by very nature of your being.

"Well, I don't like it," he says.

You benefit from it as well, as does everybody else. The small self reaps its riches in the ways he can find, whether it be through intellect or love or money. You all find ways to decide you are better or must be better than someone else. The true Kingdom, you see, is not a lie. When you have been taught that the material realm is an illusory realm, in fact it is true. But the illusions may be known in rather different ways. It is an illusion that money will buy you happiness, but money itself is an illusion. It is an idea that has taken form that you pander and utilize. It is just—understand this, friends—an idea. You would lift your life for the good of others if you could, but not if the money isn't good enough.

Here we go, friends:

"On this day we choose to realign our values to the higher accord that is present now, and in doing so, we expose ourselves, our very selves, to be revealed in the higher octave where any distortion of value may be seen, witnessed, known, and released. We say these things of our free will in the knowing that we will be met in the higher vibration of the Christ Self, the True Self, the Divine Self that knows who we are and will support us in this revelation. I say these words of my own free will. I am free. I am free. I am free."

Now we will speak about revelation that comes at the cost of being seen. You have all done this, told a petty lie, only to have the lie known. Most of you decide to become better liars so it doesn't happen again. What would happen if the need for the lie itself were eliminated? Underline that word. The *need* for the lie. To respond to this in a high way might be to say, "Well, I don't want to lie. I want it gone. Why would I have a need for a lie?" Here is the good and the bad news.

You have no need for a lie. And here is the bad news. Your entire reality is a lie, as confirmed by the small self.

Now that is not bad news for us. It's celebratory news, because the moment you all see this, you stop playing the game of self-deceit, you stop denying the Divine Self's rule, you begin to claim the Kingdom because you realize it, it is revealed to you. How is this done? We have told you already. You agree to it, and you align to it, and you claim it in manifestation, the Divine as what you are. Underline the *what*. And hear the magnitude of this word, *manifest*. The Manifest Divine does not operate in deceit, is not complicit to it, will not adhere to it, and, by the announcement "I am free," the claim of liberation in its expression denies the manifest world its purview and control over you and announces the liberation of the True Self from the agreements made that would tether her, bind him, to the lower way.

Here we go, friends. The teaching you are receiving now will be a testament to your growth and your ability to comprehend an idea that you may not have held prior. There is nothing outside of God. We don't damn the reality that you've created here. In fact, we celebrate much of it. We see you here in your encounters, doing your very, very best to learn and to grow in a way that you could not, had you not been born here. But the obligations of this plane, as announced by the collective, bind the individual and the collective to deceit in ways you don't see. To be realized or revealed as the True Self demands —underline *demands*—that what you have believed in that has never been true will be known by you in one way or another.

"What is an example?" he says.

That "I am not loved," that "I am not worthy," that "one man is better than the next," that your mortality is limited, that you do not express elsewhere. We could go on for days and days and days, but in fact where you are living is in a field of sandcastles. They may go to rubble with one misstep. The Kingdom you exist in, in lower vibration, is manifest through many needs, including the need to conquer and control, including the need to war, including the need to decide others' merit by a litany of inherited data that is fruitless and meaningless and usually cruel. "She will never amount to much. Look where she comes from." "They will never know God. Look how they pray." "We will always rule because we should."

The arrogance of these statements is appalling, yes, but you are complicit to them, and the world is created in very many ways to support separation. The Kingdom of the Divine operates in a different octave, and your alignment at this level, which comes through revelation, and the revealing of the total being to be made new, the resurrected self, if you wish, who can participate in the higher landscape, will not be complicit to the creations made in the lower vibration. Here is where you may dismay. You assume that this will be easy. "I will float up in a cloud in the happy kingdom I have arrived to, but when I wish to gossip about that woman over there, I still may do so. I know I am holy. I am the most holy one around, and especially in the kingdom, where I damn my neighbors. They should not be in the kingdom. They are not evolved enough."

The one who would utter those words would have created a parallel kingdom where she is the queen and the rest are her servants. The Divine Self is equal to all. Do you understand this? The majesty of the Divine Self that expresses in the beggar is equal to the Divine Self that expresses in the queen, and the queen revealed as the Divine Self will be humble, and the beggar seen will be magnificent. You will become equal in the divine truth that is present at this level.

"But this seems impossible," he says. "Don't give us a teaching that we cannot know as true."

My dear friend, Paul. This has always been true. The deep sadness we hold is how it has been denied. Do you understand this? This has always been true. There has never been one man higher than the next. There has never been fear controlling you all. You have acquiesced and damned yourselves and created the vehicle for the destruction of all for your demand to rule others. Do you understand?

What we are teaching you was true a million years ago, will be true a million years from now. The charade you partake in will be ending one way or another, either by offering to remove the costume, as we suggest, or having it ripped from you. When there is an explosion in the castle, the queen can be seen crawling out the window and her servants may not help her out. Do you understand this? The leveling of a reality to an equal plane finally will come in one way or the next, and your pretenses, one higher than the next, will be met through your own actions, but they do not have to be.

We sing your song for you so that you may learn the words to your true inheritance, the Divine as you, who has come to sing. As each of you raises your voice in song, the chorus is heard around the globe, and the awakening that has already begun will be known by the multitude. The revelation of the aspects of the self that need to be revealed to be anointed and seen in love, or liberated in freedom, or denied, perhaps, in a true way, will now commence. We invite you each to imagine for a moment that you are lying prone in a safe place, the most safe place you can imagine yourself being, and we allow you to know yourself here as living the life you have known, and all that you have agreed to is present for understanding. Now if you would imagine that the True Self as you is present here as well as a light in the center of your heart that is beating in a bright pulse and asks only for the permission to assume the entirety of you, if you take a moment, now, and feel this pulse, this light in your heart, and support it by agreeing to it and allowing it permission to assume you. "I know who I am in truth. I know what I am in truth. I know how I serve in truth. I am free. I am free. I am free."

And, as these words are spoken, you give permission to all that you have withheld from the light, that which you have kept in darkness, have sought to renounce and failed, permission to be seen, permission to be known, permission to be revealed and then lifted and absorbed and known again by the True Self that is present here as you. Take a moment and allow the aspects of the self, the hidden pieces, the tokens of the past and the tethers to the past that you have blamed, but protected, for your unhappiness, to be seen and known and realigned in a higher way.

Here we go, friends:

"On this day we choose to give permission for every lie that I have invested in, that we, the collective, have invested in, to be released from me in perfect ways. And through this agreement, I am guaranteed the circumstance and the support to align to the freedom of this in peace, in grace, and in allowance of my True Self in its

perfected state to be known and responded to as who
and what I am. I give permission to the life that I live to
be my teacher. I give permission to the body I inhabit to be
my teacher. I give my emotional self permission to be my
teacher. I give my mind the permission to teach me, as
well. And as all aspects of me and my life are now complicit in this great act of courage and change, I say yes to
the truth of my being, being made manifest in the highest octave I may now align to. I know who I am in truth.
I know what I am in truth. I know how I serve in truth.
I am free. I am free. I am free."

We are working with Paul. We are working with each of you
on the claim that has been made that you are in agreement
to, and the support for this encounter, we promise you, will
be ongoing until the revealed self is unbound, unburdened,
untethered to the lies of history that she has believed in or he
has agreed to, either in circumstance, belief, or knowing in
separation. The Kingdom is here, friends. It is waiting for
your entry, and we will take you there, as we may, at the level
that you can agree to it.

Paul has a question. "Is this going to be hard, what you
are saying we will have to do?"

No, it need not be hard. All that is hard is continuing to
hide from the very light that you are. Do you understand?

That is the choice you make when you stay in the shadow, and the rule of the small self. Period. Period. Period.

Day Thirteen

We each come before the master, before the divine truth of all things, with a willingness to be known. You must understand this, friends. We all stand before the highest energy, the infinite potential in manifestation that you may understand as high truth or God incarnate, with a willingness to be known.

Now, Paul is questioning already. But the manifest is not God. You use the word *manifest*. This is a teaching of manifestation, and to decide primarily that God must resemble what you assume it will is to design a God to fit your needs. We will begin this teaching again for Paul. Ask for quiet, primarily quiet for him to present according to our wishes.

When you understand that the truth of who and what you are may be witnessed by the Divine, that you may be known in fullness, you understand all things that may be known by you in accordance with truth. The willingness to be witnessed in truth, outside of your ideas of yourself and the choices made by you that affirm an identity that is not true, must be comprehended in a way by you as the requirement for ultimate transition. Understand this, friends. *Ultimate transition.* This is the resistance Paul is experiencing, and, as we said, the trajectory we bring you to beyond the known must be understood outside of the known, and all attempts to dictate what this teaching should be will be met by resistance because you will not understand the totality of the teaching with the intellect.

The assumption of the Divine as you is the practical application of the teaching you have received thus far through us. Assumption, to be assumed, is to be loved, and responded to, and known in a newer way than you can imagine with the vocabulary that you have inherited. But for this to happen, you must agree that the witness, the revelation of the self, will be re-known in a new way.

Now imagine this. If you were exposed to the light in fullness, what would be known? Anything that you have left unloved may now be loved. Anything that has been denied will now be accepted. Anything that you understand as fearful will be re-known in a new way. The juncture you stand at today is in agreement to be re-known—underline *re-known*—by those of us who attend to you each and hold the pattern of the divine truth that may be impressed in the fields that you are in agreement to.

Our nature, beyond your nature, our light, beyond your light, our love, beyond your love, may know you and assume you in the True Self that is your inheritance. The purview of the True Self is manifestation. Underline those words. *The purview of the True Self is manifestation.* What the True Self claims into form will be known in form. You may call it a miracle. You may call it alchemy. But all it truly is, is the Creator in operation, and magnificence operating as you in an assumed state. Underline *assumed state.* It is very important that you understand the difference between the small self's creations and the creation of the Divine. The hands work the needs of the small self desires. Vibration claims into form the manifestation of the Divine. Reasoning, we say, will be met by you as required to create something in form as it always has. But effort is no longer useful at this stage of realization.

When one is assumed as truth, in vibration as truth, one is a barometer for truth as may be known in expression. Underline *expression.* What is expressed is made in form. Now here is the challenge for some of you. You understand the idea that you can be assumed by the True Self. We have been teaching this for many years now. You can realize yourself in a higher octave and claim from the higher octave where you abide. You can be expressed in dominion through the claim "I am here, I am here, I am here," the Divine Self announcing itself in manifestation. But when you put all the pieces together of what this is, this is the manifestation of Christ in form and expression. The most simple way for you to understand it is you become what you have always been in the highest octave that is available to you to express as on this plane of experience. By *plane,* we mean shared plane of creation. You are not alone in this octave. In fact, you have many around you that are experiencing their world in rather different ways than you may be. So the call forward that you give to your fellows—"You are free, you are free, you are free"—claims them with you in high accord.

What is it to be here in an assumed state? It's very simple, really. It is to know yourself in union with the Divine, nothing less and nothing more. The presence of the Divine is witnessed by one who is one with the Divine and not outside of it in consciousness. Understand, friends, there is an aspect of you that is fully realized in a higher octave, always has been. The Christed Self, the realized self, the you that you are in highest expression that carries no name but I Am, the Divine Self, the what that you are in form as this, is assumed in realization. The I Am as you is your expression. This is nothing other than a new way of being as you have always been.

Understand now, friends, that when you live your life in high accord, you are still accountable to all of your choices and your creations. It is not a get out of jail free card. If you have issues that you must attend to, you must attend to them. In fact, the obligation to attend to your creations in higher mind is hurried in some ways through this passage. Imagine you have been to the tailor. He has yet to sew the pockets on your suit. You are dashing down the hallway, ready to enter the new vibration, with a tailor hurrying behind you sewing those pockets in place. You get to attend to your creations as well.

Now, we must address Paul's concerns about this teaching and this text. This text is an assumption of the reader in higher vibration. Far more than it is an instruction, it is a vibratory vehicle for expression of union. By bypassing systems of control and adherence to form, by bypassing agreements made in lower nature, by agreeing that you may be known, and aligning to it in revelation, the realization of the True Self, you align to a way of being that exceeds and surpasses what you have known in your experience thus far.

The work that we do with the reader of the text is to move her up the scale of recognition. When one is witnessed in totality, one may have the expression of it. Do you understand this idea? If we operate at the level of the Christ in vibration, what we claim and see and know is of like vibration by its being. God sees God in all its manifestation. Realization is the witnessing of God where God has been denied. Do you understand that? You realize the beauty of a child, a man, or a woman, not by looking at what they appear, but by knowing who they are. And, as we know who you are and claim you in truth, you are recognized, and revealed, and seen, and all those things that you would hide and bear witness to in fear will be revealed, and seen, and lifted, or released from you so you may ascend to your inheritance. We are not doing the work for you, you see. We do it with you, and there is a vast difference between the two. We may lift you to the light to be re-known, and you may scurry for the shadow that you have known yourself in because you believe it is safe. You may enter again to our witness when you like, but the realization of the Divine as you has been claimed.

Understand, friend, you thought you were Mary Smith's child all your life. "My mother is Mary Smith." And one day you discover that the father of Mary Smith's child is God itself. It's really rather hard to go back to identifying as Mary Smith's little girl, once you know your true heritage. Like it as much as you wish, you embroider all the towels in your bathroom with Smith just to remind yourself of who you are through the old structure, but each time you look in the mirror, you see God's child. Do you understand the teaching? You remember who you are, even when you fight it, even when you wish to wish it away.

Now Paul has so many questions about this teaching, but the one he is bringing forth is a rather small one. "But what about my personal needs? I understand that this is who I may be, but what about my happiness, or a partner, or a life I enjoy? What about the claims I require? Are they neglected in this teaching? Do we no longer want what we thought we wanted? Do we forget the old ideas of what it means to be here on this limited plane that you say we live in?"

Actually, what happens when you are assumed at this level is that the resistance to joy is released. The resistance to love, the fear of being seen, is what precludes you, and all of you, from the lives that you may really live. You think you will only get your way as the small self, and she or he is what is being assumed by the Divine in its union. Do you understand this? So the idea of being revealed and seen, all aspects of you in allowance of visibility, actually aligns you to the release of the very things that would preclude what you call your happiness.

Now your designs for happiness may change. "I want someone who looks a certain way, does a certain thing, to be by my side through this life that I live." The prescriptions of the small self will be released or unraveled along with that sweater that we spoke of yesterday. Do you understand this? The prescriptions of what should be, or have to be, in order to be known in the ways you think they should, will be released in the witnessing we described.

"Now what is the witness?" Paul is asking. "Is this what we have done already when we allowed the lies to release?"

Not yet. This is a different response. It is the teaching of union as may be comprehended by witness. Understand, friends, that you have been living in a dim room. The brightest it gets is the light that you can see in the comfort with your eyes unbound by sight. When we gift you with light, it illumines what the eyes cannot see, what the eyes could not bear. When you are known in truth, every scale of illusion must be removed from your vision, and those include the ideas that you hold dear or sacred that have never been in truth.

So what we will do now for the reader of this text, for those who hear these words today, is claim the alignment that is required for the assumption of the whole. We will do this for you by your agreement, and the creation that will be made henceforth in the field you hold will be the claiming of union as the active principle of your being. Understand this. Imagine that there is a sign being placed in the auric field announcing union, and its resonance aligns you in union as the manifestation of it, the consciousness of it, the agreement to it may be held and known.

Here we go, friends:

"I allow myself to be known in fullness. I surrender my need to be known as I believe I should be. I give permission to every aspect of myself to show itself in fullness to what I know as God or the level of consciousness that I may be met by in absolution. The name I give myself, I Am, is offered to God to be received in union, in fullness, in recognition that I am of the whole and have never been other. As I say these words, I am allowing myself to be made visible to the highest sight and claimed in the highest octave that I may be in comprehension to, and this agreement is made by me, now and forever. I am one with the Source of all things. I am one with what I know to be God. I am one with what I claim as the True Self in alignment, and agreement, and realization, and in manifestation as who and what I am. As I say yes to this, I permit all that has been hidden to be revealed and reclaimed by the God I choose to know, and I say yes, not only to the purgation, but to the reclaiming of each self that I have ever been in union with the truth of its being. I know who I am in truth. I know what I am in truth. I know how I serve in truth. I free. I am free. I am free."

Be received by us, each of you present, each of you reading this text, each of you who hears these words. Be received by us in union.

Receive God through the bodies you stand in.

Now ask this question. "Who am I? Who am I? Who am I?" And see what the response you receive is. "What am I? What am I? What am I?" And ask for the response. "How do I serve?" Understand the answer will be the expression of your life from here on in.

We have said yes. You have agreed. That was the step that was required, and the witnessing of you that we have done and claimed you in has assumed you in the octave we abide in. The octave we abide in as the Christed Self, which is what we are in truth, as are you, will be your legacy, your inheritance, and now the lives that you express through. We have been claimed as your teacher. You have agreed to the instruction, and the bells will now ring that this significant occurrence has been made so in the energetic fields that you have claimed and known yourselves through. We bear witness to all of you, and we offer you this, this simple claim:

"On this day you are wed with your own true nature. The divine marriage of spirit and form has claimed itself yet again in humanity. We are here. We are here. We are here."

Stop now, Paul. Period. Period. Period.
(Pause)

Trust yourselves, please, to follow the lead of the True Self, who has announced itself as who and what you are. Trust the alignment you have been given to operate as you. Don't fight the tide, but ride it lovingly. Be carried forward by grace and your awareness of the truth of your being as being ever present. Give yourself permission, please, to be realized each day as the who and the what.

Upon awakening, sit for a few minutes, and say these words: "I have come to know myself as I truly am in all my encounters and engagements. I have come to be realized as who and what I am in every instance of my day." This simple affirmation will claim you in the day, by intent, in congruence with the vibration you have amassed and agreed to and aligned as. The gift of the day will be to teach you what you need to adhere to the agreements that you have claimed in truth.

Absolution, you see—to be absolved of fear and the fear of the self being witnessed—carries with it temptation. We will explain this now. The sovereign self exists plurally. You are one of many incarnated beings in encounter with one another. The Divine as what you are exists independently and in consort with the Source of your being. To be in union is to know the self as at oneness with the material world and the spiritual world. You can no longer decide that you are not of the world because the manifest self existing in this expression must know itself in all experience. What this simply means is that the material experience in these encounters may call you to them to teach you lessons that you would not agree to as the old self you were.

Understand, friends, that experience does not end in divine union. In many ways, it begins anew. There is nothing to fear. The idealization of what was may tempt you often. The agreements made in fear that serve the needs of the small self will still be present in the environment that you have existed in. You must attend to these things each day you see them, and your witness of them as the True Self will be the reckoning with your reality that you require to move beyond the known.

He wishes an example. The young man has ten locks on his door because of the fear of the world beyond. These were created at a time when he agreed to separation. He enjoys the locks on the doors. They give him a sense of security that is no longer required. You may have a lock on your door, if you wish, but why do you wish to keep the world out, or yourself in, must also be understood.

The things that you have claimed in fear that have become manifest on this plane will be there to be seen, and to be seen anew, and every reckoning, every encounter with one of your creations, must be seen as a blessed event. "Oh, there is that one I sought to avoid all these years. Do I run for cover? Do I run in the other direction? Or do I witness her as she truly is through the eyes of the True Self who are unafraid?" Habit, you see, can dictate action, and you have habituated many aspects of your life that must now be rendered anew.

The Divine as what, the manifest self in this world, claims the world into being by her very presence in it. You are the wave, the echo, the resounding bell. The energetic field you hold, which has been encoded in truth in agreement to marriage in union with Source, claims all it sees in its true nature.

Revelation, we suggest, is the revealing of what was always present where fear sought to mask it. The witnessing you bring to every event that you witness claims the thing you see in the octave you now abide in. The claim "You are free," rendered to another, whether or not they know it, will liberate them from the matrix of fear that they have invested in. The ringing of the bell, the echo of your vibration, the resonance of your being does this work. You have come to sing, each and every one of you, and, as the song is sung, it is sung in the higher octave to lift the world you express through to its true nature. A new world is known, is revealed, is seen and witnessed and claimed by the one who knows who she is. Dominion, you see, is the province of the Christ.

The teaching you were given—"I am here, I am here, I am here," the Divine as you claiming its purview—was indeed assumed by the claim of mastery in freedom. "I am free, I am free, I am free" can only be claimed at the level of the Divine Self, who is here as you. So the assumption of the claim in purview, now in freedom, is what claims the world in absolution in its own way. Can you absolve another? No. But you can know them in truth, and, in your knowing, in your regard, in your claim of truth for them, you are free. The gong is rung, the bells sing out, the echo is made, and their field itself moves into co-resonance with your own by nature of your being.

An experiment for each of you today is to go to a public place and witness each one you see as what they truly are, not the who, but the what, the manifestation of God embodied in form. We have taught you who, witnessed the Divine Self that is inherent in each man or woman that you see. We have moved to the what. Witness the manifestation of God in all you witness. See form itself as re-known in the octave of truth, of freedom, of the Christ made flesh. Bear witness to the Divine in each member of their body, each hair on their head, the expression they wear, the carriage of their gait, the way they sit, the way they frown, the way they weep or smile. Witness the Divine made flesh, because the one who may do this is the one who has claimed it, agreed to it, and realized it as the who and the what that they are in truth.

As you do this exercise, bear witness to each human being and how they respond to the expression of you seeing them in witness. Make a note, if you wish, of the transitions you see. Understand, friends, you are not fixing their bad leg or clearing their tears. You are witnessing the Divine that is the tear itself. All expression of humanity is divine. Do you understand this? Suffering itself may be perceived, and re-understood, and reclaimed beyond the thing it presents itself as. Trouble, as you see it, may be rendered in a higher way beyond agreements to trouble, but it is still divine. You are not whitewashing the walls, you are not covering up pain. You are seeing God in form and flesh and incident as it is manifest with you—underline *with*—in co-resonance, vibrational accord, the divine measure that is met by the presence of the Christ made flesh in manifestation.

"Is this heretical?" Paul asks. He likes to rely upon the old teachings to give him comfort. He does not wish to disobey any rules that may have been written to keep himself safe from the pyre. We will explain this. The Christ is the Divine Self. We are the Christ as we express in this way, and you are the Christ as you realize your truth, realize and know and embody and express the what that you are. The Word made flesh, the Manifest Divine, is here to be known, and it comes with thunder and glory and light. We say yes to you in this incarnation as you know and realize the manifestations of God that are before you. Everything is sacred. Do you understand these words? The hair on the man's head, the tears of the old woman, the laughter of the child, birth and death itself are as sacred as all. Bear witness to joy, bear witness to grief, and know that all, all, all is of God.

The exercise today is to witness others in form and manifestation, the what that they are. "I know who you are in truth, I know what—*what* means manifest—you are in truth, I know how you serve in truth" may be used to support this activation in your agreement. But at this level of alignment, the manifestation of the Divine as you does not require the phraseology to claim the echo in resonance. Your very being holds it. Do you understand this? Why do you practice the scales on the piano when you have become the symphony? Do you understand these words? Why do you parrot phraseology when you have become the vowel and the consonant that make it so? How do you sing without knowing you sing? By becoming the song. Do you hear these words? You have come. You have come. You have come. And as you come, you claim a new world, and the benefactors are those who follow for eternity.

We have come in your name, in service to your being. We have come to say yes to all that is new and will be seen anew by those of you who say, "Yes, I am here, I am here, I am here."

Thank you and stop this. The exercise was given. We wish you well in your experience of the what that you are, and the what before you. Period. Period. Period. Stop now, please.

(Pause)

When we ask you to see yourselves as we see you, we offer you this advice. The ideas that you hold about yourselves, what is good or less than good, have been decided for you primarily through experience on this plane in encouragement to be as you think you should be. Any gifts you've been given or applauded for, any failings that you have been perceived as having, or claimed for yourselves, are ways of knowing the self outside of accord with the True Self. The gifts you have been given will be expressed anyway. The True Self that you are knows the highest way that a being can be expressed as. The small self's perceived failures or failings to live up to a standard of achievement, or health, or realization must be understood as agreements made in lower octaves—not the failings, but why you call them that, and there is a difference here. One man may climb the mountain well. Another may hobble on bended knees. One may climb with confidence. One may climb in fear. But you're all going up the mountain in your unique ways. The one with the confidence is learning through confidence, the one in fear is learning in fear, but the learning still is participatory to the climb upward. Do you understand this?

To judge another for not being who they should be is to decide for them who they should be, and no one has the right to decide for another. What you do have the right to do is to know who someone is in their fear or in their courage, in whatever way they present. The Divine as them, the truth of who they are, the unlimited self that is made manifest as what you are and is climbing with you, the scale of the mountain, varies from being to being. Some of you have chosen a wide path up the mountain. There are parks to play in, children to play with. You may take a rest here or there and enjoy the flowers. Some of you climb heartily, with a pickax, perhaps, yes, bringing yourself up the side of the cliff with blisters on your hands. That is not right or wrong. It's simply another way of ascension.

The claims you make for your own experiences in many ways dictate the path that you choose. Your belief in hardship may, in fact, make it hard, or your desire for hardship may give you the proof that the climb was required and beneficial to you. Each of you decides, prior to incarnation, the lessons you will learn, and the ways that they will be learned are offered to you by your expression, by your experience, by the choice to be. We make no one higher than the next, and we design an instruction to ensure that you do not either. The moment you decide that one is above the next, you have lost your way on the mountaintop and you are walking downward again. This is not convenient to the small self. It's a way of undermining your own progress and the progress of the one you judge.

What is most meritful is to sing the song of the ones you are walking with. Whether it be the easy walk or the steep climb upward, bless the ones you pass on the road, sing their song for them. Know in your heart that the path that they are taking is the true path for them. Do not condemn and do not laud another. To put one higher or lower is to lose balance on your own journey. Yes, there are those who have walked behind you, and, yes, there are those who will walk before you. And wherever you walk you will have a companion on either side, if you open to it. But this journey is the journey of every soul, every being who has taken form and knows himself as of his Source, her Source, or perhaps does not know.

The offering we give you today in encouragement is that the road is not what you think. There is no end, friends, to the road you walk. You are walking now in infinity, and while you live a life that has a structure, perhaps a meant amount of years in form, the eternal self is always journeying. Bless the journey. Bless the long ride home. Bless the truth of your being that knows that this is so, and grant encouragement to your fellow travelers. It is a privilege to be in witness of them.

The road is not so long as it is ever. When there is no finish line in sight, no destination to land upon, there is nothing to be impatient with. Do you understand this? The eternal road before you, in union with your Source, in constant unfoldment of learning and being and expression. "I know how I serve."

Dominion, we say, at this level of alignment, is always about the immediate requirement for expression, not your expression a hundred years from now, or next week, or the week after. You must claim what you require in the day that you stand in, and expect to receive what is required for your evolution to continue well.

The ascension continues. The long walk in eternity has no end. And that aligns you to infinity itself. The True Self, you see, is the Infinite Self, the one without beginning or end, the one who is, and always is, and always must be. As we say these words, as we end this instruction—and, yes, this is in the text, Paul—we say these words to the assembled, wherever they may be. Look around you, friends. You will find your fellows. You walk together in this incarnation with purpose and joy. You walk together in awareness of your own requirements, and if you are called to aid those you walk with, do so in love and in awareness of their sovereignty. The Divine as you is here, is here, is here, and will continue to be.

We thank you for this expression. When we begin tomorrow, we will talk about recognition and the design of the world. Period. Period. Period.

Day Fourteen

Each of you comes to us with a response that is required. "Will I get what I want?" "Will I become who I say I am?" "Will I realize myself in this lifetime?"

When you decide that who you are is the True Self, the Divine as what, many of those questions are gone for good. You have designed a life in accordance with a blueprint of the True Self, which simply means that the True Self is creating for you. You are no longer the magician trying to bring something into being. You are no longer the one who must make decisions from a list of possibilities that you have created or inherited.

Each one of you comes to this expression with a design. The bodies you are in, the energetic fields you hold, are in fact the design that is now being re-created in accordance with the Divine Self. The manifestation of the Divine claims you into being in a new way, and manifestation, which is where you stand today, has significant energies that must be claimed and responded to in order to be realized.

As you stand before us, as you are seen as you are, as you are realized by us as what you are in truth, you claim an identity outside of what you have adhered to prior, and the agreements that you have made as the small self are eradicated by the truth of who and what you are. The commencing of the vibration in manifestation is what is occurring in Paul as you watch him, as you see him. And, we will suggest, it is happening with you as you speak, too.

The vibration of the Divine Self, who has come to be known by the name I Am, assumes your body and the vehicle of expression, which is, in fact, the will. The will, you must understand, must be assumed in totality and in agreement with the Divine for alchemy to truly occur. This does not mean you don't make choices, but how the choices are made are so much simpler because the knowing that you now possess aligns you to what you require. So the battles over ideas, the shoulds and the woulds, will be gone as this is done because you have no need for them.

Now the ramifications of this on the lives you live will be significant, and you need to understand why. The why is very simple. You are who you say you are. "I am free" has been announced and claimed in the auric field, and the consciousness you hold has made the manifestation of the claim as an embodiment a reality for you. By *reality*, we mean manifest, and as you are manifest at this level of agreement, the claims you make on the world you see have great import.

Understand this, friends. What you say carries vibration. What you claim responds to the need of the design you witness. The world is in design, and you are in witness to it in a high vibration. The claim "I am here," the Divine in purview, the True Self seeing her world before her and knowing her relationship to it, was a requirement to the claim "I am free, I see the world before me and I know I am of the world I see, I am here." The realignment to the being of freedom—"I am free"—allows you to enter the world that the Divine Self has claimed in manifestation. Do you understand this teaching? The Divine Self in her claim "I am here, I am here, I am here" announces purview, jurisdiction. What she sees, she is in accord to. Imagine, if you wish, that there is a lawn before you. The difference between "I am here," which is perceiving the lawn, and "I am free," which is claiming the lawn, and you in it, in vibrational agreement without hindrance that needs permission from a reality that you thought could not conform to the high octave—the high octave is now upon the lawn and she is free.

This is very important for you to understand. The ramifications of choice, which we have spoken about thus far in our texts, must now be understood as very important because of what you've become. The Divine in manifestation, while it is always who you were, has not been claimed in fullness, and now it has been. Know it or not, you have done the work if you have aligned with this teaching and made the agreements to align to true will, the Divine Self as expressed by you. As a result of this, your presence in your world, by design, re-creates the manifest world by your exposure to it and its response to you.

Paul had a question yesterday. "I did what you asked us to do. I saw someone. I claimed 'I know who you are, what you are, how you serve, you are free, you are free, you are free,' and I made the focus the manifest self that was perceived, and I felt the vibration of the man respond in my field. I felt the waves of his expression respond to me."

That is the catalytic effect of the claim of truth and freedom upon the field of the manifest plane. Do you understand? When you feel the reverberation from another in response to the claim, you are experiencing the alchemy of the Divine in manifestation. Do you understand this? Your testament to this will be your own experience of the vibration and its response.

The design of the world may now be known, as well. You work with a man. Now work with many men, the manifestation of all. You work with a tree. Now work with a forest. You work with a glass of water. Now go to the ocean and claim the manifest Divine that is implicit and inherent in all things. Do you understand this? By your witness and being, in expression, your presence aligns the vibrational field of whatever you see and claim in truth. Do you understand this? The manifestation of God, the Kingdom itself, is the response you are receiving.

So Paul is saying, "Well, I just felt the man's energy field. I didn't think it was that big a deal."

Here is the big deal, Paul. Your experience is an example of the affect of the vibration made known in form. That is not a small thing. You may call a rose a rose, but until you know what a rose is, realize the rose, it is just a thing. Do you understand this? To know a man in circumstance—"There is that man I met the other day"—is vastly different from realizing him. And the claim you make for him—"You are free, you are free, you are free"—is in realization. Do you understand, yes?

Now some of you decide that the work that you have done thus far must not be true because you cannot believe that you will have the response from the manifest plane that we have described thus far, that you will not know in your own vibrational field the impact of the claim upon the field of another or a thing, or perhaps many things. You must work with this in intention. When we return, we will expound upon this teaching. Period. Period. Period.

(Pause)

We sing your song for you, and now you know the words. "I am free. I am free. I am free." The Divine as what you are has come and is claiming a Kingdom. Now the Kingdom of the Divine Self, as we have said prior, is everything she witnesses, all that she perceives. And the ideologies you hold as the small self will be released now so that true perception may claim you. Underline *true perception*, perception not inhibited by the old frames or ways of deciding what things are, based upon past prescription.

The design you are now, in form and field, has gone into an agreement with the truth of being—collective being, not just your being, the truth of collective being, which means that you can support the whole by recognition of it and its true nature. Your willingness to agree to this was the one requirement that was needed to progress you through the initiations that have been required to underline and comprehend and fully claim the Divine as what.

Now the responsibility you hold is to create your world in

a higher octave. How is this done, but through the choice to align to the divinity that is ever present, and the manifestation of it will be the response or the echo that you receive. The vibration you feel in recall, the boomerang, if you wish, the response, if you wish, from the claim that you make for another—"You are free, you are free, you are free"—will be one of the ways that you know that the work you do has been found and received in the field of the one you initiate to her true nature.

Now understand, friends. You are never overriding free will by doing this. You are never deciding for another what they should do. You are claiming what is always true, and the aspect of the being that announces itself to you in reverberation, echo, or recall is the Divine Self saying, "Yes, I am here. Yes, I am free. Yes, I am assuming myself."

Now the individual that you have claimed this for will have choices to make. The individual small self may say, "Thank you, no," and their True Self will go into waiting until the perfect moment is recognized to bring forth the individual self to a reckoning of truth. You must understand, friends, that all of humanity is undergoing this passage, and a reckoning of truth, either by an individual, or a country, or a world is a requirement now to move beyond the known structures that you have been abiding by. The claim of truth—"You are free, you

are free, you are free"—in the field of another supports the
choice to agree that will be offered by the individual through
her own expression or life experience. So never for a moment
think you are fixing someone or making them holy. They
have always been holy. All you are doing is recognizing that
for them, and letting the imprint of that recognition serve
their energetic field so that they may know it as well. The
manifestation of the Divine as what you are in form and field
is what has been done, and now will reveal itself, in the perfect ways.

Paul is requiring us to answer this question. "Did you
mean unveil or reveal?" In fact, they mean the same thing.
Our initial word was *unveil*, but the word that you heard in
its place was acceptable to us, so we did not make a correc-
tion. The alignment you hold, Paul, as the vehicle for us, is
about to move forward in a reliable way that you may not
know until you fully encounter yourself as what you are.
Now, because manifestation has been claimed and aligned to
in a significant way, your own energetic field is now assuming you, and, consequently, the physical self as the vehicle for
our expression. And our expression, we must say, is consummate with the expression of your True Self. So we work as
one because you are as of us and have always been so. So the
reliability that we teach you will be known to you, will be in

effortlessness of vocation, and speech, and alliance with the Divine Selves of all you encounter.

Now responsibility for the rest of you must be understood. You have initiated great change by your agreement here. By the acquisition of this text and your participation in this work, your agreement to hear these words, you have already decided that the being that you are is going to move forward and create itself anew. Underline those words, *create itself anew.* You don't create yourself anew. The small self cannot do that. It would be forced and effortful. But the True Self doing this in expression is an act of holiness, and if you align to the holiness of the act, the expression is not only fruitful, but perfect in all ways.

The anointing you have received has decided with you that the manifestation of this process will be known to you while you are here in form. Some of you decide to acquiesce first to the field, and then say, "Hold on, I just saw what I said yes to. I cannot handle the transformation. Let's put it on hold for a bit." And, because you have will, you may hold off for a bit, and that is understandable and perfectly acceptable. But the agreement to manifest in totality, the Divine as the what, is frankly the responsibility of each human being. And each human being will rely upon this choice to make itself known fully at one point in their experience on this plane, or some other.

The manifestation of the manifestation of the Divine, you

see, is not only a process, but an alchemical reliance upon the True Self to be the active participant in the transformation. If you were now to assume that, because you have married the True Self or merged in union with the Source of your being, everything that you knew should be changed, you would be acting as the small self. But if you understand that it will be changed in perfect ways through your own encounters with your lives, the responsibility is then placed upon the Divine, and, as you express as the Divine, you will understand your own requirements for change.

Some of you come to us with a hefty list of things you want done or transformed. In almost all cases, those lists were made in fear and the belief that these things that cause you pain may never be gone. Understand, dears, these things *are* gone at the level of the True Self, and your recognition of this in manifestation releases the claims these things may have made upon you. The choices you will make now in the higher way will be brought to you in order, and this is important that you understand this. Some of you may find that you expect yourself to be bombarded with choices, and that you will not be able to manage them. In fact, what happens is that the ball is rolled gently to you, not thrown at you, and your picking up the ball and agreeing to the ball is really all that's required.

"What is the ball?" Paul asks. Opportunity to know the self

in a higher way through relation, through encounter, through action, through being —underline *being*—finally, because everything else is always and only an expression of being.

How do you serve has been the question for so many of you. How each human being serves is by the realization of the True Self, and the True Self in expression is perfect service. But you may be called to act. The ball will be rolled to you, you will pick it up, and you will honor the call that the True Self brings you. *It will always be in support of the whole.* Underline those words. The individualized need to be seen as special, or in perfect service as the ego would have it, has been dismantled. There is no need for pride. There is no need for false glory. But there is great need for the voice to sing, to be heard in echo, and your alignment to the world that you live in is in fact the service that you provide.

When you see the stars at night, know the stars are of God. When you witness something on the television, know that each human being, regardless of what they express, is of God. When you witness a man or a woman in a fight or a conflict, know who they are in truth, know what they are in truth, know how they serve in truth, and they will be liberated in the claim you make for them. "You are free." You will feel the response or the residual echo in the field you hold as you are met by them through the intention you have set. The stars will welcome you, the earth will gift you love, and the man and the woman in conflict will align to their true nature in recognition of the claim you have made.

To deny someone else their truth is to deny your own. To deny the divinity in the stars is to deny your own. To decide that things should look the way you think prescribes a world in limitation because the thinking that you have held thus far is severely limited in what you can imagine. The True Self is not bound by the imaginings of the small self. She may conceive beyond language and know beyond form, and because she can, what she can claim into being will be new— underline the word *new*—new as in unknown, prior to expression. Once again, we say, when something new comes to you, don't seek to name it by the old, but invite it to tell you its name and you will begin a new vocabulary in expression that will surmount the old, that will express itself in vowels and consonants, perhaps, but perhaps not.

Once you understand that even your thinking is not language, but has conformed to language in comprehension, you will begin to understand that the movement beyond language allows telepathy as a gift or a simple way of expression for many of you. This is a shift in the field of humanity that is expressing itself now, and generations to come will be party to this because the way has been paved. When you are no longer limited by the ideas of how you may communicate with each other, when your reliance upon technology as the vehicle for exchange is seen simply as a tool, but a small way of knowing truth, you may know for yourselves how wonderful the vehicles that you truly hold are in availability as conduits for truth and information that may support the well-being of the species on this plane. Species, plural, yes.

Now by invitation, we have come to you—by Paul's invitation to serve, and his invitation to grow, and by your invitation to be taught. So as we commune with you today, we have a few things we wish you to know about our role in all of this. We are not just teachers. We are the Christ consciousness. You may call us Melchizedek. You may call us the one with no name. It matters not to us. But our field is actually enveloping this plane to support its alignment, and each of you, as you agree to this work, supports this plane in the higher way. We don't make ourselves special. We simply be in the octave we know, and lift you to us so that you may sing for your fellows, just as we sing to you. The reverberation you feel when you claim another in truth is what we feel when we witness you each and we know who you are. The gift you give us is far more than you know. We are humbled by your willingness, and grateful for the reliance you have upon the True Self you know to be your instructor. We are your temporary teacher. Please understand this. The Divine within, the True Self, the Christed Self that you truly are is your true master. We are gifted to play the role of instructor while you need us to be present for the shift on this plane that we know is occurring. But we say these words to you: Honor your truth. Do not bow to us. We are simply love. We are simply expression. We are simply expression of the Divine in language and love and vibration that you may know.

We will suggest this teaching complete itself for the day. We have much more to teach you. We will say that this is the end of the chapter, yes, that we began yesterday or the day prior, and we will say, yes, thank you for your presence, and good night. Stop now, please.

Chapter Eight

HOW DO YOU CREATE A WORLD?

Day Fifteen

Trouble comes when you decide for yourself that you are vulnerable or accepting of trouble. Understand what this means. The idea of trouble itself is an expectation that can happen. "It was trouble" is an affirmation of the quality of experience you had. "She is trouble" is an expectation of her behavior. "There will be trouble if and when" is a decision about the future. And, in all ways, when you render yourself available to this, you call it to you in energetic ways.

The trouble you expect may not manifest as you see, but the energy that you project remains in your field until it is released by a higher way of being. When you lower your vibration in expectation of trouble, you decide for yourself what you have claimed. No one has done it for you. You have chosen and finally agreed to the nature of the experience that you would emblemize as trouble.

Now why we say these words is not only for Paul, who has his own worries about his life and relations, but all of you, as well. As you are moving into a new encounter of being in your lives, post productive act of union, the realization of the marriage of the True Self through you as you are must become seen evidentially in your experience. You need to know, in some ways, what the monikers are, what the ways of being are that you may attend to as a result of the work you have done. The engagement in the old becomes more troubling. The memory of a painful event, when it arises, can be used productively if you realign your system in a higher way that re-creates you outside of the memory. The memory is only an idea that you have attached to, as is trouble, an idea that you give meaning to and claim in certain ways to have a certain effect or experience here.

When you align as the True Self, you are still attending to the creations you have made in trouble or in fear throughout your lifetimes. The manifestation of the Divine as you, while it has claimed you in fullness, has not necessarily claimed the artifacts of a life that surround you now. The home you return to, the job you go to, the poor neighbor, the good friend, the old enemy may still be present in the forms you have known them through. How do you attend to these things from the higher way?

The first thing we must say is you are not who you think you are anymore. You are who you thought you were, perhaps, in a memory, but that is not who you are anymore. The realization of the True Self in re-creation as you has announced itself as free, and the obligation of the energetic field, in response to this, is to create the being that you are in freedom of expression. Freedom of expression means how you are known and expressed in all ways and in all things.

Now the memory of pain, the memory of trouble, in its own way may be understood as a photograph in an album. "This is me when I was two. That was me when I was five. This was my family on that trip." There is a neutrality, perhaps, to the witnessing of these things as the True Self. The memory may be present, but the attachment to the pain of the time, or even the joy, may be understood as something that was, not something that is recalled or reclaimed in the moment you stand in. We don't void the memory. You align to the memory from the high perspective of the True Self that does not instigate the emotional reaction or feeling that you have utilized to know the self through data or past events.

When you choose this realignment, the photo album is present, as is the one who took the photo, which is, in fact, you.

The maker of the memory is the one who takes the photo, and what is impressed by the maker of the memory—"That was a lovely day," "That was the worst time of my life," "That was the worst thing that could have happened"—in most ways serves to reclaim the vibrational identity of the event as was assumed originally in memory. And much of what you remember is only your imprinting well after the fact of what you think was so.

As you obligate yourself to re-creation—"I know who I am in truth, I know what I am in truth, I know how I serve in truth, I am free, I am free, I am free"—you sort through the experiences as they emerge and align to them as you are today, and not as you were prior to this encounter, with this vibrational octave. Imagine you are singing a high C and the memory exists in a much lower octave. Your return to memory as was claimed by you at the time it was claimed, and then embellished in fear and worry, will call you back to the lower octave, and from that place you realign to the creations that exist in consort with that vibration. For example, you are in recrimination. "What that woman did to me" calls you to recrimination and the response to it in all ways. Do you understand this?

The Divine sees the Divine in all things. The injured party may see injury wherever she looks when she is complicit to that vibration as a way to self-identify. "I am the one who was injured." We don't say you were not. We say it is not who you are, and there is a great difference between those two ideas. Realization, the revealing of the True Self at the cost of the known, is a peeling away, in some ways, of the accruements of history and time that you have thought to be you, yes, but also those things that you have attached to by agreement or affirmation that they should be there because they were always there.

So here is the big question. How does the merged self, the one in union, the one who has chosen realization, attend to history? Here is the simplest answer we can give you—in knowing that she is not history. Always, the idea of self-identification will rule in this regard. You are the one, perhaps, that made the error in judgment that caused you some pain. You are not an error in judgment. Do you understand the difference? The understanding that something happened is vastly different than re-creating it as armor or a wardrobe that you must wear to remind you of the terrible thing that you have known yourself as.

Paul is seeing a scarlet "A" emblazoned on someone's blouse, and that is a perfect example of one wearing their shame, or deciding for themselves who they are, based upon what they think that they have done. When the community emblemizes the "A" upon someone's blouse, the community is at fault and operating in fear and in negation of the Divine that exists beyond the act that has occurred, not the individual who has to suffer the consequences of the whole.

As we speak to you about what you are, and how you continue to live a life on this manifest plane in a higher regard of assumption of the True Self of those aspects of you that would have been denied otherwise, we support you each in making this journey a *loving* one. Understand this word. There is no trial that can be faced by you that cannot be met in the higher agreement of the True Self as you reclaiming what she sees in the higher octave that you have aligned to. Our return to history in this teaching is to tell you that history itself may be reclaimed and re-known in high alignment by the one who knows who she is. The disregard of history, the pretending it didn't happen, is not supportive of this. The re-seeing is, the revelation is. The inherent Divine that is implicit in all action can be understood, in some ways, as the opportunity to remake all things.

Now Paul is discouraged and confused. "The inherent Divine in all action. I can think of many actions that are not divine. Murder is one. Hatred is another. Is there truth in these things? Is there divinity in these things?"

What you are talking about is the expression of an individual or a culture in action that is in denial of their divinity. Understand this. Anything that you could name that is horrific to you, given the morality you hold, is a clear demonstration of the denial of God, or the fear of God, being expressed in terrible ways. When we say these words to you, we want you to understand their true meaning. The True Self is implicit in any individual and every individual, regardless of what they have done or claimed, and the issuance of an act is an issuance made in fear, and to agree to the fear—"that terrible thing, that horrible thing that cannot be blessed"—is to claim power in that thing and elevate it to a force that you might call evil. Evil is a creation of man in this stead, and the Divine must be present in everything or it can be present in nothing. How can you have them both? When you decide that anything can be forgiven, anything can be known anew, you have progressed to the incarnation of the Christ in manifestation.

Regardless of the work we have done with you, which is to assume you in truth, you have many things that you would choose to claim in horror or outrage and deny the presence of the Christ in. How is this remedied? The witnessing of the landscape that we were instructing you in is the clear answer. The response by the frequency of the object, or the individual, or the terrain, or the situation to the claim of truth will be the acknowledgment of this effectiveness of claiming. When you claim upon a battlefield—"I know who you are in truth, I know what you are in truth, I know how you serve in truth, you are free, you are free, you are free"—you are claiming the battlefield in its divine nature, and the residual response that you will experience will be testament to the realignment of the molecules themselves of everything you are addressing. Alchemy, yes.

"Does that make them put down their swords?" Paul asks. Perhaps not, but your realization of the divine presence—"I am Word through what I see before me"—reclaims the divine truth and lifts what you see to its being and expression at that octave. Only the one who sings the high note can lift other things to the resonance of that sound. Do you understand this? At the high note's vibration, there is a claiming that lifts the lower to it. You will not lift the atrocity, the battlefield, the hatred, the prejudice, the famine, the war, and the greed by climbing into the mire of it and attacking it with a knife. You will not find your way out. Do you understand? By rising above it and claiming it anew, you may lift it to the Christed Self to be seen, to be known, to be revealed in a new way. We teach you re-creation through revelation and knowing, and, if you understand that this is to be done by the True Self, and not the small self who would blame or injure or pound the table in his anger, you will comprehend that the Divine as you is the one who renames the world.

"Renames or reclaims?" Paul asks. They are both the same thing. When something is renamed, it is known anew. To emblemize something as atrocious solidifies it as what it has been called, and when you all claim the thing in atrocity, it builds itself to greater form. The clay that you all hold as manifesters is impacting the initial structure and growing it through the negative attention that you have compounded it with. Do you understand? Re-creation comes when something is reclaimed, re-known in a higher way. If there is a child named Joan and the next day she is called Alice, we promise you that Alice will know herself differently than Joan did. Now while this is a cosmetic example, it is also true. When something has been decided upon in language and claimed again and again and again, it is known in form as solid, in solidity, impactful solidity. These are the things you don't imagine can ever change.

When something is re-known and re-seen and reclaimed from the higher octave, it may be made new. The solidity of form is not existent in the same way in the higher vibration. Do you understand this? You are moving out of density, so realizing the inherent divine that exists in something in low vibration reclaims it in the higher where it may be remade. Return to the clay. You all impact what you see by the consciousness you hold. You are all making something as if from clay by your relations to it and your announcement of what is what.

In the higher octave, you operate in the same way without the density because you are not claiming in fear. Do you understand this? Where there is no fear, there is grace, and the magnitude of the Divine may express itself quite easily. The Divine Self, the what that you are, is participant here, not the small self who thinks she should know how a government should be run, a school should be run, a policy should be made, or her neighbor should behave. That would be the codification of the small self's agenda upon what she witnesses.

As you agree to the what that you are in assumed form, the vehicle that you stand in, the body and energetic fields, are in alignment to support the reclamation of all that exists in form. Do you understand this principle? Because the body is now known as the Divine Self in manifestation, everything that exists in form may also be understood at the same level of expression. You are not above other things. You are witnessing the Divine that is inherent within, and that is the process from this stage of vibration, of reclamation, and reaffirmation of truth in all things.

Now as we complete the teaching this morning, and this is the beginning of a new chapter, yes, we would like to commend each of you who hears these words for your participation in this teaching. Wherever you stand, wherever you be, we nod our heads to you in gratitude. In a moment, we may take some questions on the teaching, but first we say thank you. Period. Period. Period.

Q: Does this claiming need to be done with acute focus, or can it be happening with the song of our being?

A: Both are so. Now acute seeing requires discipline and intent. If you understand it a little bit differently, it takes no effort on your behalf to see a butterfly go across the room. You know a butterfly. You are simply saying, "That's a butterfly." You are realizing the fact of the insect as it propels itself forward. The Divine as you does not struggle to see the Divine in anything, so there is no struggle, there is being. Focus is different. To give something focus is to give the attention to the butterfly and acknowledge it in accordance with, so this means your realization of the butterfly is confirming the vibratory accord. The Divine in you witnesses the Divine as the butterfly. That is simple focus. The moment you try to make the butterfly divine, you are self-defeating because you are denying the butterfly's identity and trying to make it something it is not. Remember, always, you are claiming what is, not should be. Thank you for the question.

Q: So when I witness a horrific scene on a battlefield, somebody being slaughtered, bleeding, and then I claim it for my True Self, the divinity in this being that's bleeding and being slaughtered, how does it look? Does it look beautiful?

A: You're asking for something impossible. Once again, the teaching is the same. The realization of the dying man is the realization of the True Self that has taken form and is in an experience. It doesn't condone the experience or the battle. Do you understand this? You are not making it God. You are seeing the inherent God through what has been denied as God, which transforms what you see. Can you imagine, in a plague-infested town, where nobody received their blessings because the preacher could not attest to the Divine that could exist in those poor people? What a horror that is. The preacher leaves them to die because he has decided that God could not inhabit such a man or woman, and it is too dangerous for him to be in that encounter. The realization is that the Divine is present in all manifestation, regardless of whether it appeals to your liking. Do you understand this? Some of you think if it is God, it must be pretty. That is not so. God is in life, in birth, in death, in blood, in feces themselves. You cannot say God is in some things and not others. The Divine as what you are witnesses the Divine upon that battlefield, the inherent truth in the dying man, and in the one who holds the sword above the dying man. You don't exclude him, either, or you will be playing favorites, and God does not. If there is a God, and we suggest there is, he loves them both, it loves them both equally. The murderer and the murderer's victim are loved equally. Now you can't imagine doing this because you are bound to the history and the years where you hung the poor murderer in the town square so the town could be absolved of the incident itself. And the creations that you have used to know God in many ways will design for you your experience of God. To realize the Divine in the battlefield is to go against all the pictures of the lilies you might see. God is in the lilies, and God is in the blood that falls upon the lilies in battle. Period. Period. Period.

Q: Just clarification. So event is not identity and need is not terrible, so that if one on the battlefield is hurting, that in itself is not terrible, it may call a response of more love, but it's not declaring it not divine and still there can be a need?

A: You realize the Divine in what you see. You are still trying to make it good or evil. If you go that route, you cannot attend to this teaching ever. It would be impossible. You are back to the idea of a God in a cloud who favors some above the others, and when misfortune comes you must deserve it or there must be no God at all. When you realize anything in truth, all you are being asked to do is witness the presence of the Divine that is inherent in all things. It is not to condone the action. Go attend to the man on the battlefield. Hold him in your arms. Love him if you can. Mend his wounds if you can. This is not passive. God is in the bandages, and in the blood. The Kingdom, as we said so many times, is the awareness of the Divine in all things, not just the things you like. As you align in the higher vibration, things are lifted and reclaimed. That does not mean people don't die, or become wounded, or have trouble that they experience. It does not mean those things. It does mean that how you experience them must be very, very different than the small self has chosen.

We spoke of trouble early in this chapter as a way of understanding that your complicit nature to any event is happening through vibration. If you understand that while we give you examples of war, war itself is a creation of fear and nothing more than that. What else could it be? Fear is a lie. We're not saying that there is not a war. We are saying that your realization of what you know as war can be re-known, and reclaimed, and re-made in the higher octave. In the higher octave, where you now abide in vibration, you don't claim in war because you don't operate in fear. Do you understand the teaching? You may say yes, if you do. [Yes.] Question, please.

Q: Sitting here today I realize that I'm having a very different experience with the teaching. In the past I think my practice would have been to try and expand my capacity to tolerate the suffering or the pain or the fear and be able to hold it, but it feels now a neutrality of there is no capacity to hold it because

I see it in a very different way. There's more of a neutrality to be able to witness all of it from a different place.

A: You don't deny the suffering of another. You don't leave them in pain. You don't attend to them through fear. You know them in love. Now love is neutral in some ways because it has no conditions. When something has a condition, it is not neutral in the least. To realize one in suffering is to love them dearly. Don't misunderstand this. The understanding you require is that as you witness the one suffering, you realize them beyond their suffering. You don't make it better, or condone what they feel. You lift them by virtue of your presence and the names you give them. "I know who you are in truth, what you are in truth, how you serve in truth, you are free, you are free, you are free." Thank you for the question. One more question, please, on the teaching.

Q: This type of witnessing that you are talking about—is this what you have always meant about how to witness something without being complicit?

A: Yes, exactly. By not going into agreement with the pain, or confirming the pain, by which you lower yourself to that agreement, you support the other in moving beyond it. You don't deny the pain. You are not pretending it's not there. And by *agreement* we mean going into accord with it. If somebody is saying, "I've been terribly hurt, look at the terrible things that have been done to me," and you go to them and you say, "Yes, you are a victim, what terrible things you have endured," you are confirming the fear and the lower identity that has been claimed. You don't deny that the event has happened. You do align to the truth of the person who is seeing herself as a victim to lift her beyond that state through your witness. If you go to confirm her in her suffering, you support the suffering. Do you understand this, yes?

That would be it. We will take a pause. Thank you all for your presence. Stop now, please.

Day Sixteen

We tell you each that the lives that you have lived thus far need to be justified by you. There are no mistakes in life. There are opportunities to learn. Some may not be very fun, very agreeable, but all are required on this journey you take together. If you decide that an event in your life has ruined your life, you have empowered the event to the degree that it will claim you forever in its purview. An event is something

that happened. It is not who you are. And your realization
of who and what you are will actually reclaim memory in a
higher octave.

So much of what you remember is how you interpret, and
embellish, and reason, and wish. So much of what memory
is, is a confabulation of what you think should be there. The
reason you do this is that you invest in incident and claim it
in import by value. Understand, friends, that all value is, is
the degree of investment you bring to anything, any occurrence, high, low, or in-between. One of you decides that this
is an important event, and most likely everybody will go into
agreement with you. The reason for this is that, culturally,
you look to others to show you import—the fashion of the
day, the way a thing is done, a way to realize the self in congruence with somebody else's idea.

When you have a tragedy in your life, you also have an
opportunity to realize yourself as independent from the incident. While the incident occurred, you were transformed by
your engagement with it, not by the incident itself. Do you
understand the difference? You are transformed by your relationship to the incident and the investment you give it, not
the incident itself. The incident itself is something that happened. It happened, you agreed that it happened, and you
impose upon it the meaning that you give it, which then relies upon you to reinvest it every time it is encountered.

When there is a loss, you understand the loss, you grieve the loss, but your intent must be to realize the self beyond the loss. You have been informed by the incident only to the degree that you have decided that you should be, and much of this is done by cultural agreement. "She should be grieving forever." "He should be ashamed of his behavior forever." You create systems that you use to impose morality upon one another, and what morality really is, is once again the collective endowing something with meaning.

If you understand that a promise kept has value, you understand the promise of value and the meaning that value has. When you understand that a broken promise is only as important as the meaning the promise was given, you will have an understanding of this teaching. Whatever you see before you in the life you are currently living is being agreed to by you, and you invest in everything you see as you think you should, or as you were taught, or as the collective would have you. When you realize yourself, first as independent from the collective, and second, not reliant upon the meaning things have been given by others, you will begin to realize yourself outside of the claims made for you or by you in history. Realization of the True Self as the who and the what that you are will do this with you.

Understand, friends, that the True Self in her realization makes all things new. Underline those words. *The True Self in her realization makes all things new.* And what was seen in fear, or in frustration, or in anger will then have the opportunity to be re-seen in the higher octave that you abide in. You have become so used to claiming things in fear that when you do this you often associate it with reason. "I had the right to do this." "Anyone would do this." "She would be a fool if she didn't." And as you agree to fear, and give it purview, and announce it's present in what you see, you claim a world in fear.

How do you move beyond a world in fear? By re-creating it at the level of agreement where fear cannot exist. This cannot be done by the small self. Do you all hear these words? The small self cannot re-create a world in a higher octave because she abides in a lower one. This is not a bad thing. It just is what is. The True Self, you see, exists without fear, or blame, or the need to antagonize, or the desire to control. Do you understand these things? When you are doing any of those small things, you are doing them as the small self, who is always doing his or her best to have her needs met in the ways that she thinks that they should.

As the True Self emerges and begins to reclaim you, the first thing you will notice is that what you see is not what you thought. "I thought this was important, but it is not." "I thought this was meritful, but perhaps I was wrong." "I perceived myself as needing this or that, but I no longer feel this."

As the fabric of your reality is beginning to be transformed, what actually occurs is a realization of what has always been. The cost of the new is in fact the release of the old, and all the old is, is what was superimposed or obscuring the truth that was always present. The Kingdom, the realization of the Divine in form in all the material realm, is present now as it can ever be. Do you understand this, friends? It is here as you are, but may only be witnessed by the one who knows who he is. The True Self enters the Kingdom at the cost of the old.

Now what does it mean? Do you have to sacrifice? Do you have to relinquish? Do you have to pretend you are not who you were? Absolutely not. You do unbind and unattach, and what is relinquished or known anew are those things that you thought you were that perhaps were never true. And the values you hold, which have been impressed to you culturally through familiar ties and the decades you have lived through, will also be understood in rather new ways. Your investment in truth will become apparent the moment you realize that you are a great beneficiary of it. You have believed that lies would protect you, but they keep you hidden from the light. You have used lies to make agreements with yourself and your fellows. You have created institutions that trade in lies, governments that utilize fear to control you. When you stop agreeing to fear by agreeing in truth, you realize yourself in relation to all these systems, and consequently are no longer in coherence with them. By *coherence*, we mean vibrational accord.

Now the reason we say these things to you now is that the dissolution of much of the material realm, as it is re-comprehended, will allow you to re-create in the higher octave that you now perceive through. To understand this teaching is actually to understand that matter is malleable to conscious thought, and how something is seen and given value is making it so. By *dissolution,* we mean when you stop investing in a lie and you value in truth, the creations of lies, those things made in fear, must be re-known and reclaimed. And this will be done—underline *will*—through the True Self, who actually has the ability to work as manifester in this vibration. *Manifester* is the word we use, yes. You are always creating from the known.

As you align to the value of the freedom you hold now, you have permission to conceive of the unknown, the unmanifest, and call it into being. Remember the example we gave you, that a chair may not only be a chair, but the wood in the fire. Anything created may be known in a new way. All the reliance you have upon the old has brought humanity to this precipice of destruction. You understand this, yes. All of the wisdom of the ages are still present and ignored in the face of man's need to dominate itself in many forms. The ideas of treason, the denial of the Divine Self, the ideas of rule, that you can truly control another, are creations of fear that must now be met in a higher way. This will be done, we say, by the energy of truth that is present on this plane and is engaging all. And the benefit of this is that everything that you see and can imagine seeing, finally, we say, will be in truth, and in truth a lie will not be held.

Now to re-create a world you need to have vision, but the vision the small self holds is the accumulation of historical data. While it is helpful to know how to hammer a nail and how to build the house with the hammers and nails you have, there are other ways of being, other ways to build, other ways to assume a reality beyond what's been taught to you. And our hope for us in this exchange is that we may teach you the requirements for manifestation in a way that you may attend to. A new world is known, we have to say, through realization and reclamation of the manifest that is present in the higher octave. Nothing can be claimed until it's first known in potential. And what the True Self can claim is what has not been manifest. It does not rely upon the old dictates, the old language, the old ways of being. It can reach beyond to the new that has not yet been made manifest.

As each individual rises in divine union, in re-creation, she becomes complicit to the manifestation of the higher realms as may be expressed in this plane of expression. Every vibrational field has its own accord and its own alignment that may be seen and known and experienced. As you move to the higher octave, up the scale if you wish, the resonance of your tone claims itself in agreement to the octave that you know yourself in, and this is where creation occurs. "How Do You Create a World?" would be the title of this chapter, and the responsibility to each individual to manifest a world will be made known by them through the choice they make to go into coherence and vibratory accord with that which has not yet been made known.

As we work with you, as we witness you, as we sing your song for you, we lift you to the awareness of what now may be known outside of the claims made in history. And, as we journey with you forward, and higher and higher to the unmanifest, the making of the world is simply the creation of the Divine that is inherent in all things. How a world is known and seen by the True Self is so very different than the small self that was complicit in the creations of fear that surround you. Every opportunity that you can imagine has been presented to humanity again and again and again to change its values, the meanings that it has impressed upon its world that you see before you. We have come again in order to say,

"Yes, it will be done." But realization at the cost of the known will have to be understood as the requirement for change.

As you hang on so desperately to the who that you thought that you were and reclaim what you thought you should claim, you must understand that the True Self waits in abeyance until you say, "I am willing." The moment you move into accord in the alignment of the will and know the self as free— and *know* means realize—you align to the potential that freedom brings you, and the new opportunities for manifestation will be made known to you in an instant.

We will say this again for Paul. What this teaching is, is an alignment to the requirements of manifestation. And, as the requirements are made known, they may be implemented instantaneously. We will continue only for a few more moments. Then we wish to attune them to the teaching that they are receiving. Paul is asking, "Is this in the text?" This is part of a section in a chapter on creation. We will leave it at that for now.

As we bring attunements through to the readers of this text, we want you to understand that all you really have to do is know them as true. The claim is made with you. Your denial of the claim, or disagreement to it, does not make it not so. The intonation itself will support your vibratory field in its expression, but to push it away, as if to push the salt shaker away from the plate upon the table, does not mean the salt shaker is no longer there. You are simply keeping it away by your choice.

If you align to the truth of this statement, your reclamation, the being that you are in the high octave that can be supported in the remaking of a world, will be understood, and the tools required will be made known to you. The final tool, we would suggest, will be the nature of your being, and the resounding song that the field that you hold brings to all it encounters.

You may say this after us:

"On this day we choose to realign ourselves to the highest level of collective agreement to know the work before us. And, as we say these words, the readers of this text, the students of this work, we afford ourselves the availability and knowing required to remake ourselves in coherence with the requirement of a new world. As I give my consent to know and to be in service at this level of agreement, I align my entire being to the support that is needed in order to make this so. I am here. I am here. I am here."

Now align to this potential. The one that you are who has been known will be re-known. The one who has claimed and believed will be reclaimed and known again in a higher way. The one who has seen will see a new world in the agreement that has been made. We know who you are in truth. We know what you are in truth. We know how you serve in truth. You are free. You are free. You are free.

Stop now, please.

Day Seventeen

We ask you each to respond to yourselves on this morning we share together. "What is my need? What is my desire? What is the one great wish I would claim if I could? What could I have if it were still a possibility that I had not decided would never be?" What is the true wish of your heart and how can it be claimed?

We will tell you. In the knowing of who you are in union with the Source of your being, the manifestation of your heart's desire may be rendered to you and claimed and received by you as you say it. But understand what this means. To claim your heart's desire is to give up your heart to a desire that must be claimed, and to give up your heart, you must be willing to surrender it to the unknown.

The idea of the heart's desire, that it will come to you, be folded into your heart, cared for or cherished gently, is actually not what happens. The offering of the heart, the extending of the heart in its vulnerability, in its nakedness—"Here is my heart, oh Lord, bring it to its wish"—calls you forth to a great unknown.

Ask each one if they are willing to offer their heart to its desire. When you do this, you are claiming the heart as the ambassador of the desire. The heart goes before you, un-ashamed, in its request to be met in love or in honor or in truth. The heart goes before you, aligned to its desire, and you have accepted that the heart will do what it requires, make itself known as it needs to, to fulfill itself.

The protecting of the heart, the hiding of the heart, the secret heart's desire that never sees the light, is never truly articulated because it is never exposed, is what we are teach-ing you now. And the offering of the heart, the extended heart, the heart as the gift to God in the understanding that its desire will be met, is the teaching of the morning, and the gift of the time you stand in.

As each one of you announces your desire, sees it in your heart, emblazoned with words if you wish, if you wish in song, or in hope, however you wish, the heart's desire in the heart must then be extended by you in an offering. And by *offering*, we mean it is not your business to get your heart's desire met. It is the gift you give to God or the universe to be fulfilled. In this honor, the honor of gifting the heart, the most precious thing you have, to be offered for realization and fulfillment, you are surrendering all aspects of yourself to the realization of the heart's desire.

"I offer my heart, and what is required for the fulfillment of this desire will be claimed for me, and, as I know this, as I say yes to this, I am called forth to meet it in completion."

Now the surrender that this requires is enormous. The heart's desire, the true heart's desire, is God's wish for you. Do you understand this? And the realization, the granting of the wish, is the resounding call, the re-call, if you wish to call it that, from the wish to the Creator and to you again. The announcement is made, "I know who I am in truth, I know what I am in truth, I know how I serve in truth, I am free, I am free, I am free," and the heart's desire is forthcoming to be claimed by the Divine in its issuance of its own response.

We do this with you now, one and all. Ask them this. Are they willing to name their heart's desire? Are they willing to name it and see it written on their heart? Let them do this as they will. Let the heart's desire be known and inscribed or spoken to, announced, at the level of the heart. Now allow the heart to be extended from your body as if you hold it in your hands in offering. See the heart before you, exposed, aware, vulnerable to its need, and let the need be met by the Source of your being. Respond to these words: "Am I willing to know, and claim, and receive my heart's desire?" Say yes, if you wish, and release the heart itself to the Divine Source of All Things to be met with a whisper, "yes, yes, yes."

Now the heart has been gifted in offering, its desire claimed, and now you allow, and you allow the willingness of the entire being that you know yourself as to receive itself in agreement to the desire, to the wish that was claimed. Allow every being of yourself, every aspect of yourself, every article or idea you have ever ascribed meaning to, to participate in this claim, to be in its receipt. Let the longing be ended, and let yourself be known in love.

We ask you these questions now. When your heart's desire is returned to you, will you receive it in fullness? Will you accept it in grace? Will you allow for it to be so at the cost of what you may have claimed in its place for many, many years? Will you say yes to the transformation that is needed to fulfill your heart's desire? If the answer is yes, you will go on a journey of reception, your heart before you, no longer hidden, its desire seen, no longer revoked, your love known as available to be known by another, and the gift you give in love, your heart's desire, will be given to you in response.

We will allow you each a moment now to be received by the complete vibration of your heart's desire. Be at one with it. Receive it. Say yes to it. And rejoice in its response.

"I give my thanks now to all that is for the ability to know and to claim and to accept and to receive. I give thanks now that what was in secret has been brought to the light. And I give thanks now that the realization of my true heart's desire has been met in agreement to be realized. I know who I am in truth. I know what I am in truth. I know how I serve in truth. I receive my heart's desire."

We will take a pause, now, yes. This is in the text, yes. Thank you each for your presence. Stop now, please.

Day Eighteen

Now we welcome you each to what we hope will be the next chapter of the lives that you live. Each of you comes to us with an awareness of who and what you think you are, and the realization of the self, the Divine as who and what, has been this teaching, in sequence, since we first began. Our instruction, the realization of the Divine as what, the manifest self, the truth of who you are in full expression, has been this teaching and will continue to be. And we want you to know that the assumption of the self, the small self being assumed by the divine what, by manifestation, realized and encoded in full expression, has commenced in form. This includes all of you who have been undertaking this class and have been deciding to come with us every step of the way.

There has been a sequence to this teaching of realization which involves a consent by the small self to acquiesce to the fullness of the Divine that is her birthright. As the small self is reconceived or assumed by the action of God—or your own true nature, if you prefer—every piece of you involves itself in this reintegration as truth. Underline the word *as*. There can be no aspect left that you leave outside the light, that you hide from the sun, that you cast away in shame. There can be no aspect of you that is aligning to fear and claiming fear as her God. There can be no aspect of you who decrees in shame, who announces his name in fear, or greed, or complicit nature to manipulation. There is no way that the True Self can express as this, so it will not.

The aspects of you that you have assumed to be fraught with fear have been brought forth through this instruction, and reclaimed and realigned in the higher octave that the Divine Self expresses through. And the consequence of this is that the alignment you hold in high octave manifests as the what that you truly are for the purpose of re-creating a world, reclaiming a world in agreement to truth, a world that is not fraught with fear, that does not lie, that does not hunger to be fed by fear, but knows herself as one with all things. The Divine as what you are knows herself in union, and claims a world in accordance with that knowing. The one in union realizes a new world, and to be in union is to be assumed by the True Self, who has come to bear witness to the manifestation of God that is inherent, implicit, present in all manifestation.

Now the glory of God, if you wish to say it this way, can be found in anyone and anything, and the testament to this teaching will be how the world is rendered in a higher octave as a result of your being in it. The testimony of the work that we have done with you will be your own expression, the manifest self, the one who has come to be expressed and to express in resonance and vibrational accord at the level of Christ consciousness.

Now to be at this level, and to sustain it, is to reclaim yourself in the authority you hold as the divine truth has been expressed by you, to surrender to it, and to claim it in courage in the face of all that would say no, that would discard the inherent truth of the divinity that is present in all, the realized self, the one who has come to sing, to pronounce her name—"I am free, I am free, I am free." And your response, the individual's response to the agreement you have made to incarnate at this level of agreement in manifestation, is the announcement of the Divine that is now present for reclamation, agreement, and joy in all things.

Each of you comes into a lifetime with an agreement you have made to be learning, and acquiescing, and choosing the lessons that will claim you in realization. Each one of you says yes to the ideal of the truth of your being, but the manifestation of it in form and field in many ways has been denied you by your agreement to fear, which means your alignment to it, your engagement with it, and your false assumption—underline *false*—that you cannot be without it. The Divine as what you are is fearless. Do you understand this? To be fearless is free of fear, and to act in the face of fear, to surmount it, which means to rise above it, is the gift you get of claiming your truth in authority, the Divine as what, the manifestation of God in every cell of your being in its alignment and agreement to sing all its wisdom, all its love, all its expression as may be known through you, the miraculous you who has embodied in the higher light of the Divine Self.

You all come with an agreement. You say yes to it, and, as we have been called to cry yes to your agreement, to sing yes to your desire, to say yes, you have come, you have come, you have all come to the altar in divine union to be realized in fruition of the what that you are, the manifest self, the Christed Self, who can only come as you. Hear these words, friends. The Christ can only come as you. You are the vessel of this, and your agreement to align, incarnate, at this level of assumption is the foretold Christ or the realized self embodying for the good of all. No one is left behind. Hear these words, friends. As the chorus begins to sing louder and louder and louder, the echo of the song in vibration scales the globe, aligns the globe, receives the globe in all its manifestation to come to the alignment of the True Self, the presence of the Divine that is inherent in all.

We sing your song, yes, because we can teach you. But you must teach your fellows that idolatry of fear claims a fearful kingdom, and the light that you are can say, "No, I will not. No, I cannot. I know who I am in truth. I know what I am in truth. I know how I serve in truth. I am free. I am free. I am free." The freedom from fear, fearlessness, is the incarnate self that may call others to her that may bear witness to a new world.

When you say these words to your fellows, "I know who you are in truth, I know what you are in truth, I know how you serve in truth," the echo of the claim you have made will assume you again and again in your own field. Each time you align another through this claim, the recall or the reverberation of the God self within the one claimed will meet you, and in a way that you may know. The alignment you hold now through this engagement is what claims you anew, and the new self is the one in authorization who may claim these words for anyone. Underline *anyone*.

Each day you leave your home, each day you look out your

window, each photograph you see, each image you see of another, know who they are, and in the claim of what—"I know what you are," with that as the agreement, the what that they are—the manifest self will send you back in her field, in his field, the consent, the alignment, and the recognition that they have been known. The God within them is what sings back to you, and you will know it.

The creation of a new world is what we teach now in this chapter and in texts to come. The manifestation of God in form has been your instruction, and freedom from fear, the liberated self, the one who claims "I am free, I am free, I am free," is the one who says yes to this step, this agreement to claim a world anew. We are telling you the truth. Your very presence at this octave of agreement supports the alignment of all you encounter. The energy of your being in its reverberation, its echo, its alignment, and its response to all else that is manifest, will be what does this. The small self's mind does not inherit the Kingdom. The True Self does, and the entryway is before you.

We are inviting you all now, each and every one of you who hears these words, to step across the threshold into what is now present. See us, if you wish. We are many. We are in prayer all day, all night, at all times for the assumption of humanity to its awareness of its true nature. And we will call you forward and greet you each in honor of your effort, of your surrender, of your willingness, if you will allow us to. Step across the threshold. Come to the Kingdom. It is here, we are here, and we are honored to sing your name—"You are free, you are free, you are free."

Come, if you will. Come in song, come in laughter, come in prayer, come in wonder, come in joy, come in grief, but come. Come join the chorus we sing together for the reclamation of a new world beyond fear, beyond tyranny, beyond doubt, beyond the names you've claimed and the heresies committed by denying the innate Divine in your brothers and sisters, in the manifest world itself. See the Kingdom, see the presence of the Divine that is here, that is here, that is here at the octave we sing to you at. And one by one, a million by a million, come and join and claim anew. A new world is born by your very witness.

The teaching we are giving you now is in preparation for where we take you next—re-creation and manifestation as may be understood by you through alchemy and insight. "Why insight?" he asks. Your realization of the inherent Divine in manifestation reclaims matter and aligns all things to the higher octave where all exists in truth.

Everything you see has been given a name by man. The rock and the sea, the sky, and the stars, and the earth have all been named. And, as we say yes to the inherent Divine, the manifestation of the Divine that exists in all matter, we lift the world to the higher octave where all will be made new. New, new, new. Understand this, friends. To be made anew is to be re-created in higher alignment. The fear-based self has been assumed, agreed to, received in fullness. And as she sings and extends herself to realize herself in the material world through how she perceives and reclaims in agreement to the inherent Divine, her witness is her prize. And the gift of sight, of insight, of seeing God as the star, as the earth, as the rock, as the tree, and seeing all who dwell in their beauty, will claim her in fullness. She becomes one with the stars, and the earth, and the rock, and the tree in realization of her union. You exist as you, and beyond you. You exist in form, and beyond form. You exist on this plane, and beyond this plane, as all do in the higher octave.

Our teaching has always been union, and fear has precluded you from the gift of it for far too long. The alignment that is present now has been agreed to. The resonance of the chord that is being played now, through this teaching and all who attend to these words, will be the vehicle of transformation for all who encounter it. You become, not the teacher of the work, but the expression of it. And the field that you hold, in its echo, in its reverberation, expresses itself as the new world is called into manifestation.

There is no doubt here at this level. There is no agreement to fear. There is comprehension of what has been known, what was chosen, what was learned through. And understand, dears. Your learning continues, all in all in all, through all time. Your expression as this supports the demonstration of wisdom and claiming freedom for all you see. At the highest level, dears, all of humanity is free. At the highest levels, loves, you have never been enchained. The small self in her alignment agreed to many things. Many have been learned through. All were opportunities to learn. But, as we say yes, those days are ending. You are here, and, in the highest way, as the True Self, you have always been free.

We will end this chapter now with this prayer.

"On this night we choose to welcome all who will come across this threshold to glory. On this night we welcome each who have committed to the yes of their assumption and realization as the True Self. And on this night we say yes to all who will follow you through the door that has been opened by your agreement."

Paul, we will say these words to you now. The door has been opened. You too may walk through. We thank you each for your presence, and good night. Stop now, please.

EPILOGUE

Day Nineteen

We ask you questions now about where we go from here. We say *we* intentionally. We are your teachers, yes, but we shepherd our students in the ways that they ask to a common destination. There is one God, one Source of all things, and, as you know yourself as what you are, as you realize yourself beyond the fear that you've claimed, what you may understand and become is the self that has always known her truth, that has always stood in glory, and will be a testament to the vibration of God simply as you are by nature of being.

You come to us, you see, with one request—to be liberated from fear in order to know, in order to realize what exists beyond it, and the triumph of this teaching will be the remainder of your lives, if you agree to the teachings we have offered you thus far. There is no man born, no woman born, who comprehends the importance of this until they are in an encounter with their own divine nature, and, in fact, assumed by it. To be assumed by the divine nature, to be the one who knows in her embodiment, in his recognition of his true nature, makes one a light to the world. And her expression, his being, is a way-shower simply by her essence, his recognition, in manifestation and alignment for the benefit of all.

On this night, we support you in a new claim. "Who am I beyond what I have known, and what will I do with the world that I know as I move beyond it, as I see the creations of man before me? As I recognize my complicit nature to all of these creations and become willing to move beyond them, how do I know myself? How do I comprehend my fellows? How do I choose anew that I have aligned beyond the fear that perhaps has claimed me in fullness until now?" The ideals you hold of what things have been are actually being transformed now by collective agreement, and the manifestations you see on this plane are all in change as humanity awakens to what must come, what must be seen beyond the idealization of form that you have chosen.

If you only see one thing in this text, in this teaching, let them be these words. You are known by us beyond what you have known, and humanity itself will be re-known in the higher octave through their agreement toward realization and materialization of the Divine Self that may be known and claimed, comprehended, and aligned as. Because of this, the world you see is being reclaimed, and the memory of the old one day will be scattered to the winds as the new takes form.

You all want to know what happens to the world you have known. What happens to the world you have known is that it is re-known, re-comprehended, and re-understood by the true nature that you have qualified as by nature of your being. And, in comprehension and agreement to the new, the new will be claimed in a higher octave than you have believed possible.

Now Paul is fighting this teaching. "But what does that look like? What does it look like in form? What do our children discover, and their children's children? What is the world they inherit?"

Every generation confirms the world they live in. You must understand this. And the dictates of every generation, the things made into form by the collective or individual, become an artifact in some ways, or a legacy that is inherited by those who follow. What you are claiming, the students of this text, the students of this teaching, is the higher awareness that will support the next generation in a new realization of what it means to be human, what it means to be the Divine, and how you may exist in your Divine Self in encounters with others in an awareness, or agreement, or realization of truth.

So much of what you've seen and believed to be real is artificial, is an idea, a creation of humanity that has taken form and been chosen to learn through. As you are embodying in a new way, the ideal of manifestation must also be reclaimed, and the one who announces himself—"I am free, I am free, I am free"—becomes actually free of the collective fabric that has been chosen in prior times to inherit a new form that may be realized by the collective. It is not just a jump in realization. It is a new regard of what you are, who everyone is, and what now may be claimed by the collective. Your choice now is to inherit the Kingdom, to realize it, to know your participation in this, not only for you, but for those who will follow you and decide with you that what you know and what you can know may not be in deceit, may not be in collective fear, may be in a knowing of your birthright, the Divine as what you are, and as all are, as well.

Each generation contributes to the knowledge that may be received by those who follow, and the generation you stand in, all who are born and may know, chose to embody for the purpose of the escalation of humanity. In spite of what it appears, in spite of what you may see, you all said, "Yes, I will come, I will see, I will grow, and, as I become aware of the what that I am, as I claim my true nature, as I align to what I am and realize a world that operates in vibrational accord, I gift what follows, I gift who comes after with the awareness of their own nature."

If you can imagine a time without language, you can understand the importance of language in transforming a world. You have all been blind in many ways to the Divine as what, and the circumstances of your time are actually relaying you with the requirement to grow beyond the known, to develop beyond the known. What you perceive of as trials are always opportunities. You are used to this on an individual level, but you cannot fathom an entire species moving into a confrontation with what they have denied, which is their own true nature, the monad, the Divine Self, the Christed Self, the Logos, the truth of your being, and the truth in all things. In this awareness, in this confrontation with the material realm in conjunction with what is now available in the higher octave to be aligned to and witnessed with, there is an acclimation, or upsurge, or rebirth of the species itself in a new awareness.

Go back to that time when mankind existed without language, and imagine yourselves now at that juncture. As we have taught you, you move to a new language, a new way of being expressed, a new way of regarding the whole that has not existed in manifestation in form thus far in the lineage that you have known yourselves as. The great step, the high octave, the alignment to be, composed in a higher key and expressed as that music, is what is here. You are listening to the overture, and nothing more. The times you stand in, as we have said, are a time of reckoning. And a reckoning, a facing of the self, the collective self facing its creations, are offered an opportunity to be reclaimed, reborn even, in higher awareness.

Do not decide that what you have known is what you will know, because the changes that come at times of great change in some ways void the old. Your participation in the reclamation of the Divine Self in form and field is done for the whole. You become the note that plays and is heard, and the energetic fields of all that you encounter are in a residual response, as they are understood by the knowing that the vibration you hold attaches with. Imagine a bell that has a song, and the song is heard each time the bell is rung, and everybody who encounters the vibration of the bell is absorbed by the sound, and, in that encounter, the awareness is instilled in them of their individual requirements for the knowing of the who, and the what, and, finally, yes, the expression of what they are.

The true nature of humanity has, in many ways, been precluded from full expression through false teachings, a disrepair of doctrine that was initially rendered in truth and later corrupted. The violation of the sacred pact of humanity and its Divine Source is being remedied, and re-known, and reclaimed, and the celebration that will commence when you move beyond these times of change will be a thing of joy.

Now the times you stand in, as we have said, hold great change and great promise, and also the potential for destruction. You must understand that, when a thing is destroyed, it may be remade on a new foundation. A faulty house may only be prepared for habitation for so long before you must return and rebuild the foundation that the beams were placed in. Everything is in transformation now, and please do not be frightened when systems fail, or what you thought should always be there no longer is. All it is, is the potential of the new making itself known through the debris of what is now passing.

So he interrupts. "But what if the new is not good? The old house was fine. Perhaps the roof leaked. Perhaps it needed new windows. But it was still a habitable house."

The houses you live in, the structures you know, were built to support you and your agreements to fear. And, as we have taught, everything made in fear, known in fear, claimed by fear, must be reclaimed in a higher way. So don't despair when what you have counted on seems to be passing from you. Celebrate the new, and align to the potential that what is being claimed anew will exist in a higher octave and be expressed at the level of consciousness that humanity can attend to.

"It doesn't seem," he says, "as if humanity is transforming."

We see you rather differently. We comprehend your investment in the known. But the vast nature of the potential that is seeking reformation, reclamation, will not be missed by any of you. And your True Selves actually comprehend the necessity of the transformation that you are undergoing. Humanity itself has a will, a collective will, and humanity itself has said, "Yes, we are free, we are free, we are free." And, in that announcement, the cages of old, the deceit that has kept you at bay or controlled by others, is being released, sometimes easily, sometimes with a cry, but the cost of freedom is the reliance upon the cage you have been living in. You cannot be in that cage and sing the song of freedom anymore. You are here to be known, to be seen, and to speak the Word of truth to all you see. You are here to support the others who follow you on a new road, a high road, a magnificent road to your own potential, and the potential of all, in a new way, in beauty, in truth, and in the awareness of the divine union that is your birthright, and the birthright of all.

As we conclude this teaching, we must discuss where we wish to take you. As the world is changing, the requirements for being in it require explanation and understanding. And in the texts that follow, we assume you, not only as a student, but as a teacher to support those who will come after you in their awareness of their truth. We are completing this text, and as we intend to make ourselves known, we say thank you each, thank you for the blessing of your being, thank you for your attention to these words, and thank you for the gift that you are giving to those who will come after you.

We say thank you. We say good night. We say, yes, this is the end of *The Book of Freedom*. Period. Period. Period. Stop now, please.

ACKNOWLEDGMENTS

Dustin Bamberg, Tim Chambers, Joan Katherine Cramer, Mitch Horowitz, Amy Hughes, Jeannette Meek, Victoria Nelson, Noah Perabo, Amy Perry, Brent Starck, Natalie Sudman, and the Esalen Institute.

ABOUT THE AUTHOR

Born in New York City, Paul Selig attended New York University and received his master's degree from Yale. A spiritual experience in 1987 left him clairvoyant. Selig is considered one of the foremost contributors to the field of channeled literature working today. He offers channeled workshops internationally and teaches regularly at the Esalen Institute. Also a noted playwright and educator, he served on the faculty of NYU for more than twenty-five years. He is the former director of the MFA in Creative Writing Program at Goddard College and now serves on the college's Board of Trustees. He lives in New York City where he maintains a private practice as an intuitive. Information on public workshops, online seminars, and private readings can be found at www.paulselig.com.

"Charming . . . Miss Potter's life story, the attitudes of the Edwardian period, and the struggles of engaging individuals of differing social status skillfully blend history, mystery, and fantasy."
—*VOYA*

The Tale of Briar Bank

"With each succeeding volume in the series, Albert's voice grows more confident—and more reminiscent of Potter's. If you're seeking a sweet, gentle story of village life, this one will beguile."
—*Richmond Times-Dispatch*

"This whimsical, amiable, enchanting, gentle, and charming tale . . . It succeeds on many levels and for many audiences."
—*Booklist* (starred review)

The Tale of Hawthorn House

"Charming . . . The whimsical blend of romance, mystery, and nostalgia will keep cozy fans happily entertained."
—*Publishers Weekly*

"The story is a feat of writing skill that fits people—and anthropomorphized animals—into a fantastical world that the reader believes in wholly."
—*Mystery Scene*

The Tale of Cuckoo Brow Wood

"Enchanting . . . A delight from start to finish."
—*Publishers Weekly*

"Those who, like Albert's heroine, champion the benefits of dreaming, imagining, creating, improvising, and fancying will find themselves happily absorbed."
—*Booklist*